'Parents and professionals need to listen to the voices of autistic transgender and non-binary people as well as the professionals who support them. We can then share the journey together with acceptance and authentication.'

– Dr. Tony Attwood, Minds and Hearts Clinic, Brisbane

'This book is an excellent, inclusive and helpful resource on neurodiversity, gender diversity and intersectionality. Highly recommended.'

– Yenn Purkis, autistic and non-binary advocate and author

'This collection articulates – with nuance, care, and determination the multi-faceted issues faced by autistic transgender people in accessing gender-affirming care. The authors host a robust discussion of autism and gender at the intersections of race and age. This volume is an essential resource for professionals in education, psychiatry, and medicine.'

– Rua M. Williams, Assistant Professor, Purdue University

'This is an excellent resource for professionals who work with all autistic people. As Kourti reveals, gender variance is far more common among autistic people so it's important to learn how to be safe for transgender and non-binary people. Academically rigorous, accessible to professionals from a variety of fields, and written by the leading experts – autistic people themselves.'

– Maxfield Sparrow, editor of Spectrums: Autistic Transgender People in Their Own Words

'I cannot emphasize enough how important this book is, particularly in centering the voices of autistic trans and gender diverse people, rather than allistic cisgender people speaking on their behalf. A must read for educators, therapists, health care providers, parents, and anyone else who engages with these populations.'

– Dr. Shanna K. Kattari, Assistant Professor, University of Michigan School of Social Work and Director of the [Sexuality | Relationships | Gender] Research Collective

T0271550

Working with Autistic Transgender and Non-Binary People

of related interest

Supporting Trans People of Colour
How to Make Your Practice Inclusive
Sabah Choudrey
ISBN 978 1 78775 059 3
eISBN 978 1 78775 060 9

The Autism Spectrum Guide to Sexuality and Relationships
Understand Yourself and Make Choices that are Right for You
Dr Emma Goodall
Forewords by Dr Wenn Lawson and Jeanette Purkis
ISBN 978 1 84905 705 9
eISBN 978 1 78450 226 3

The Autistic Trans Guide to Life
Yenn Purkis and Wenn Lawson
ISBN 978 1 78775 391 4
eISBN 978 1 78775 392 1

Sex, Sexuality and the Autism Spectrum
Wendy Lawson
ISBN 978 1 84985 631 7
eISBN 978 1 84642 112 9

Asperger's Syndrome and Sexuality
From Adolescence through Adulthood
Isabelle Hénault
ISBN 978 1 84310 189 5
eISBN 978 1 84642 235 5

Working with Autistic Transgender and Non-Binary People

RESEARCH, PRACTICE AND EXPERIENCE

EDITED BY

Marianthi Kourti

Jessica Kingsley Publishers
London and Philadelphia

First published in Great Britain in 2021 by Jessica Kingsley Publishers
An Hachette Company

1

Copyright © Marianthi Kourti 2021

A CIP catalogue record for this title is available from the
British Library and the Library of Congress

ISBN 978 1 78775 022 7
eISBN 978 1 78775 023 4

Printed and bound by CPI Group (UK) Ltd, Croydon, CR0 4YY

Jessica Kingsley Publishers' policy is to use papers that are natural,
renewable and recyclable products and made from wood grown in
sustainable forests. The logging and manufacturing processes are expected
to conform to the environmental regulations of the country of origin.

Jessica Kingsley Publishers
Carmelite House
50 Victoria Embankment
London EC4Y 0DZ

www.jkp.com

Contents

**Part 1: THEORY at the Intersection of Autism
and Trans and/or Non-Binary Experiences**

1. Introduction   9
   Marianthi Kourti

2. 'Here Comes Trouble': Autism and Gender Performance . .   25
   Damian E.M. Milton

3. Beyond 'For Your Own Good': Youth Liberation,
   Disability Justice and the Importance of Autonomy
   in the Lives of Autistic Transgender Children   33
   Shain M. Neumeier

4. Autistic Cognition and Gender Identity: Real Struggles
   and Imaginary Deficits   49
   Reubs J Walsh and David Jackson-Perry

5. Trans, Autistic and BIPOC: Living at the Intersections
   of Autism, Race and Gender Diversity   71
   Taylor René Kielsgard and Lydia X.Z. Brown

**Part 2: WORKING at the Intersection of Autism
and Trans and/or Non-Binary Experiences**

6. Implications for Practice at Gender Identity Clinics:
   Working with Autistic Transgender and Non-Binary
   Individuals   89
   Isabelle Hénault

7. Reflections on the Spectra of Autism and Gender
    Identity: Considerations for Professionals Supporting
    Autistic Transgender and Non-Binary People 107
    Wenn Lawson

8. Developing a Good Relationship with an Autistic
    Transgender or Non-Binary Person as a Professional 125
    Marianthi Kourti and Ella Griffin

**Part 3: LIVING at the Intersection of Autism
and Trans and/or Non-Binary Experiences**

9. Autism, Gender Variance and Alexithymia: Overlap,
    Implications and Recommendations for Practice 141
    Alyssa Hillary-Zisk and Jo Minchin

10. The Resonant Self: Masking, Scripting and Precognition
    in Autistic Transgender and Non-Binary People 153
    Lexi Orchard

11. Doing Gender on My Own Terms: My Life as an Autistic
    Transgender Woman 165
    Olivia Pountney

12. The Experience of Gender Dysphoria from an Older
    Autistic Adult: Implications for Practice. 177
    Wenn Lawson

    Contributors 187

    Index. 195

Part 1

THEORY at the Intersection of Autism and Trans and/or Non-Binary Experiences

Chapter 1

Introduction

Marianthi Kourti

The purpose of this book

Autistic transgender and non-binary people have received increasing attention in recent years. There have been reports about the increasing referral rates of autistic people to gender identity clinics, the higher rates of trans and non-binary people among autistic populations, and the possible reasons that this overlap may occur. The purpose of this book is to present a variety of perspectives on autistic transgender and non-binary people in order to help those who work and live with them to understand and support them better. It also aims to provide autistic trans and non-binary people with the necessary resources to advocate for themselves, situate their personal experience in a broader social context, and help bridge barriers of misunderstanding with those around them.

Throughout this book, both autism and gender variance are considered forms of divergence that need to be understood from the perspectives of the individuals themselves; therefore, autistic interpretations have been placed at the forefront. Autistic transgender and non-binary people know who they are and what they need, and everyone whose work is for or about them should listen to their perspectives and work alongside them in their journey of self-discovery, however unconventional this may be perceived to be. This book does not engage, therefore, with any arguments that debate the existence of autistic trans and non-binary people or the validity of their experience; rather, we have created a collection of resources that will help in the process of building positive relationships with them, and help them express their needs and validate their experiences. This book presents a variety of perspectives and approaches this subject in an interdisciplinary (from the perspectives of various academic and professional disciplines) and intersectional (considering the unique social locations created by certain combination of identities) way. Autistic transgender and non-binary people will need support from a variety of people, services and professionals throughout their lives, both directly and indirectly, from teachers and parents to academics and policy makers. This book, therefore, will be of use to a broad range of people, no matter what their relationship to autism and gender variance is. It is worth noting, however, that this is very much an emerging area of study, and therefore not everything related to it can be or has been included. We ourselves are still learning and evolving as society evolves around us.

In this introductory chapter, you will first find an overview of the concepts discussed throughout the book, so that even if you are relatively unfamiliar with them you will be able to follow along. It starts with an overview of what autism is and how it has come to be understood in recent years. It then highlights what gender variance is, and presents some of the main concepts, approaches and terms around gender and gender variance, how they are commonly used and what they may mean. It goes on to discuss how autism and gender variance interact with each other, before presenting some of the more recent debates around autism and gender identity in general. It then discusses autistic transgender and non-binary people and the specific intersections where they are situated. It also provides an overview of the current politics and policies around trans issues and disability, and how these may affect autistic transgender and non-binary people as a group. Finally, you will find an overview of the book, giving a brief explanation of each chapter's themes and how each chapter fits in the overall framework of the book.

Autism and neurodiversity

The question of 'what autism is' has become a heated one over the years, with different approaches adopting widely differing definitions.

In the *Diagnostic and Statistical Manual of Mental Disorders* (*DSM-5*) (American Psychiatric Association, 2013) for example, autism is defined as persistent deficits in social communication and social interaction across multiple contexts, and restricted, repetitive patterns of behaviour, interests, or activities, currently or by history. It also states here that symptoms must have been present in the early developmental period (but may not fully manifest until social demands exceed limited capacities or may be masked by learned strategies in later life), that symptoms cause clinically significant impairment in social, occupational or other important areas of current functioning, and that these disturbances are not better explained by intellectual disability. This is the psychiatric, medical approach to autism that is predominantly used to diagnose individuals with an autism spectrum disorder.

Many autistic individuals, however, have a different approach to autism. Rather than seeing it as a pathology that causes communication deficits, they see autism as a form of neurodiversity (Singer, 1999). For them, autism is a variance in perception of the world that is monotropic (Murray, Lesser & Lawson, 2005), which includes an intense focus on interests and passions that can be maintained for long periods of time and may appear restricted to a neurotypical observer. Autistic people also highlight their sensory differences, which are only included in the diagnostic criteria of autism in the *DSM-5* (American Psychiatric Association, 2013) as a difference in perception and processing of sensory input that diverges from the neurotypical norm. They have also challenged the predominant psychiatric assertion that autistic people lack 'theory of mind' (the ability to predict and interpret the behavior of others), noting instead that non-autistic people may struggle to empathize with autistic people as much as autistic people may do with non-autistic people, framing this difficulty in mutual understanding as 'the double empathy problem' (Milton, 2012).

These autistic perspectives and approaches are the ones predominantly used throughout this book. The theories themselves are presented in more detail throughout this collection. If you are primarily familiar with neurotypical-led, clinical literature on autism thus far, much of the terminology that you will find here might be new to you. To begin with, we use primarily identity-first language (IFL) on autism (i.e. autistic *people* rather than people *with* autism). We do this for a variety of reasons; first of all, many of us use IFL to refer to our autistic experiences and understanding throughout our lives, and therefore it would be disingenuous not to do so here. Second, it is the preference of the majority of the autistic community (Kenny *et al.*, 2016), whose experiences we seek to present and validate, and using language and terminology here that does not allow for this would be counterproductive. Finally, and crucially, our own approach to autism is in line with this language use; we do not see autism as something that is, or can ever be, separated from one's existence and personhood (Brown, 2011; Sinclair, 2013). Autistic people are, and need to be, treated as whole people, valid in their own way, with their autistic ways of being inseparable from who they are as a whole.

The terminology used to describe non-autistic people also follows this framework. Whereas some authors simply describe them as non-autistic, others use terms such as allistic or neurotypical. Although these terms are often used interchangeably (at times unintentionally) to mean non-autistic people, they have different meanings. The world allistic is derived from the Greek word *allos* (which means other, just like the words autistic and autism are derived from the word *autos* which means self) and is used to describe people who are not autistic. This may include people who are otherwise neurodivergent (such as people with attention deficit hyperactivity disorder (ADHD), dyslexic people), people who are otherwise disabled, and people who are neither of those things. The word neurotypical is used to describe people who are not neurodivergent, people whose neurotypes fall within what may be considered the 'average' range. This means people who are not autistic, dyslexic and don't have ADHD, and so on. This includes other disabled people; not every disabled person is neurodivergent, although many are. Some people may describe themselves as multiply neurodivergent, meaning that they are divergent in more than one way; for example, autistic *and* having ADHD *and* dyspraxic, or any other combination of neurodivergence.

Gender, sex and gender variance

Gender variance is another broad umbrella that encompasses diverse forms of gender identity and expression. In short, people who are gender variant do not fall neatly in the socially constructed categories of male and female, man and woman, with their accompanied presentations and expressions. This, however, leaves a lot of room for interpretation; for one, gender expression in particular is heavily, if not entirely, socially constructed and will vary from culture to culture and from community to community. Furthermore, it does not, in and of itself, define gender variance. It might be appropriate, therefore, to first consider what we mean by gender if we are to define gender variance.

For a term that is so widely used, gender is challenging to define once it comes under scrutiny. The distinction between sex and gender originated from early 20th-century feminist writings as a way to separate the cultural societal practices (that may differ from culture to culture) from traits that are biologically determined, which are referred to as sex. British sociologist Ann Oakley defines sex and gender thus:

> 'Sex' is a word that refers to the biological differences between male and female: the visible difference in genitalia, the related difference in procreative function. 'Gender' however is a matter of culture: it refers to the social classification into 'masculine' and 'feminine'. (Oakley, 1985, p.16)

According to this definition, therefore, sex precedes gender, resides in the body, and is related to procreative function. This is a definition of gender and sex that many will accept as unproblematic and universal. This does not, however, mean that it has not been questioned. Delphy (1995, p.5), for example, asks:

> When we connect gender and sex, are we comparing something social with something natural, or are we comparing something social with something which is also social (in this case, the way a given society represents 'biology' to itself)?

Biologist Anne Fausto-Sterling (2012) treats sex and gender as elements that interact and influence each other in many areas of development. She argues that the creation of gender and sex does not have a starting point: biological and societal factors interact with each other from conception, when chromosomal sex is created, all the way to adult gender identity, when, arguably, one's sense of selfhood and understanding of one's own sex and gender identity are solidified. It also goes further than that, to be found in historical understandings of both gender and sexuality, cultural practices that go beyond shaping the lives of every individual human, as well as complex biological processes, the understanding of which is in part dependent on the fallible human concepts of knowledge that are used to interpret physical phenomena.

It can be argued, therefore, that sex and gender as concepts are only universal and unproblematic if they remain unquestioned. Once questioned, one can quickly surmise that they are concepts rooted in heteronormative and sexist ideas about what men and women are or are supposed to be: people who resonate with the gender that was assigned to them at birth, as well as its accompanying gender presentation, expression and social roles, who then grow up to develop affections for people of the 'opposite' gender/sex, get married, have children, and thus continue the cycle.

It is also worth noting that even established research often has muddied definitions of what gender and sex are, or even uses those two terms interchangeably. A look into research on the alleged gender differences between autistic men and autistic women will confirm this (e.g. Hallady *et al.*, 2015; Rivet & Matson, 2011; Werling & Geschwind, 2013).

Transgender and non-binary people do not identify with the gender assigned to them at birth. Transgender and non-binary are both umbrella terms with significant overlap; in other words, many transgender people are non-binary, and many non-binary people are transgender. Broadly, transgender people are those whose gender identity is different from the one they were assigned at birth but may still be binary; that is to say, they may be a woman despite the fact that they were assigned male at birth, or they may be a man despite the fact that they were identified as female at birth. The reason that the terminology 'identified' or 'assigned female at birth' is used is to highlight that gendered socializing starts from birth, and to reflect that this is how people are identified on their birth certificate. Non-binary people identify with a gender that is neither male nor female. Despite what was assigned to them at birth, they are neither men nor women, and may rather be a gender that floats between the two or they may reject gendering altogether. Some non-binary people see themselves as transgender, whereas others do not. It depends on their perception of their own gender identity as well as how they perceive the concepts of transgender and non-binary as a whole; all transgender and non-binary people agree that they experience the world differently from people who are cisgender (a term used for individuals whose gender identity matches the gender assigned to them at birth).

Transgender and non-binary people show their gender identity in various ways, broadly divided between medical and social transition. Medical transition includes interventions in one's embodied primary and secondary gender characteristics, such as hormone replacement and gender-confirmation surgeries. These can vary according to someone's needs and experiences of gender dysphoria – the feeling of distress that comes with an embodied gender identity that is different from one's sex-related bodily characteristics. Social transition includes steps to rectify how one's gender is socially perceived, used and determined, such as a change of name to one that is usually perceived as masculine, use of feminine or neutral, gendered pronouns, changes to clothes and appearance (haircut, facial hair, etc.) as well as legal documents that include one's gender identity, such as a birth certificate. These changes will depend on one's preferences, dysphoria, and gender identity, and are made to alleviate one's experiences of gender dysphoria and to improve mental health, a generally desired outcome of gender transition (Connolly et al., 2016). Gender identity is also independent from sexual or romantic attraction, which refers to the kind of romantic relationships an individual may have or wish to develop.

Autism and gender: theories, autistic perspectives and the neurotypical gaze

Since the inception of autism, its diagnosis and prevalence have been gendered. Epidemiological data has shown a higher male-to-female ratio, which recent studies place in the range between 3:1 and 5:1 (Baio *et al.*, 2018; Matson & Kozlowski, 2011; Rice *et al.*, 2012). This was historically accompanied by various theories that aim to explain this gender ratio by making a variety of claims around gendered brains, the most widespread one being the Extreme Male Brain theory (Baron-Cohen & Hammer, 1997). This theory argues that the characteristics of autism are the extreme version of a neurologically typical male brain, by presenting research on the general population that discusses the differences between male and female brain functions. However, as discussed throughout this book, this is a widely unpopular theory among autistic people and one that is considered to be damaging to autistic transgender and non-binary people, particularly autistic transgender women.

Research on autism and gender has, therefore, traditionally been formed around neurotypical perceptions of what both autism and gender are. The traditional diagnostic criteria have been mostly based on how autism presents in young boys (Dworzynski *et al.*, 2012), which has affected both cisgender women and transgender and non-binary people alike by ignoring autistic presentations that might be more prevalent among them. More recent research on autism has focused on the so-called female autism phenotype, investigating how autism presents in girls (Bargiela, Steward & Mandy, 2016), and noting that autistic girls present a more internalized autism profile which includes a more subtle presentation, the masking of many autism symptoms, and interests that are more typically female (Wilkinson, 2008). This type of research does not take into account how autistic individuals themselves view gender identity and is, again, based on neurotypical perceptions of autism. Research that aimed to preserve autistic perspectives (Kourti & MacLeod, 2019) found that autistic perceptions of gender identity are far more diverse, and put interests, rather than gender identity, at the core of autistic people's identity perception. Furthermore, autistic people often state repeatedly in their accounts how confusing and emotionally taxing 'doing gender' is for them, explaining why they may explicitly reject being confined to traditional and binary gender norms (Davidson & Tamas, 2016).

Autistic transgender and non-binary people: life at an intersection

It is unsurprising, therefore, that in recent years particular interest has been shown in the link between autism and transgender and non-binary identities. This correlation has been observed (e.g. George & Stokes, 2017), although attempts to address it have been notably cisgender and neurotypical, starting with the assumption that being neurotypical and being cisgender are, and should be, desirable states, whereas being autistic and transgender/non-binary is a combination of often arbitrary and inconsistent deficit traits that are used to invalidate one, or both, of these identities. This leads to autistic transgender and non-binary people often not having their identities taken seriously, and not being believed or given the support they need in their own terms. This is why this book was created: to address these misunderstandings, challenge these perceptions, and give professionals who work with autistic transgender and non-binary people a framework to help these people in an understanding and validating way.

Politics of transness: how they may impact the people you work with

It should be noted at this point that transphobia towards all transgender and non-binary people has been on the rise recently, particularly in the UK. One recent decision from the UK's High Court, for example, decided that children under 16 are unlikely to be able to give informed consent and therefore will need a court order to receive puberty blockers, even with parental consent (BBC News, 2020). This makes it impossible for the majority of transgender children and adolescents, including those who are autistic, to receive gender-affirming care when it is needed most. Furthermore, the rise in the media of 'gender critical' figures and voices has given legitimacy to perspectives that consistently de-legitimize the perspectives of trans and non-binary people, often using invalidating and paternalistic narratives explicitly centred on autistic transgender and non-binary people as individuals incapable of making their own decisions about their own bodies. It is important to remember, therefore, that these attitudes will affect all autistic transgender and non-binary people with whom you work, to varying degrees, and may increase their anxieties around experiencing discrimination, ensuring physical and emotional safety, and accessing trans-affirming care, to name but a few. It is important for you as a professional to understand the broader context of the experiences of those you are supporting in order to be able to build a trusting relationship with them.

Overview of chapters

This book is divided into three parts, which all interact and overlap with each other. In the first part, the reader is provided with a selection of concepts that will be useful to them in the process of engaging with autistic transgender and non-binary people. Although this part, like the rest of the book, includes some personal experiences as the majority of the authors throughout the book are autistic and/or transgender/non-binary, it primarily aims to frame their experiences within broader concepts that a professional should keep in mind when working with autistic transgender and non-binary people.

The second part focuses on professional practice and relationships. It aims to give professionals working with transgender and non-binary autistic people some practical guidelines for building those relationships, areas to explore and consider, and practical steps to take in order to optimize their support.

The third and final part highlights some aspects of the experiences of autistic transgender and non-binary people. Although more personal than the previous sections, it is not purely autobiographical. Rather, it focuses on aspects of the embodied and social experiences of autistic transgender and non-binary people that are less frequently taken into consideration by those supporting them, as they may be less well-known and discussed in existing literature. Taken together, the chapters in all three parts of the book provide an overview of many useful areas for discussion, exploration, and self-reflection for those working with autistic transgender and non-binary people.

Following this introductory chapter, in the second chapter of Part I, Damian Milton gives an overview of the predominant sociological theories both around autism and gender that help reframe autism and gender variance outside pathologizing frameworks. He presents some of the main autistic-led theories on autism, mainly monotropism and the double empathy problem. He then moves on to give an overview of sociological approaches to gender and how these may overlap with the divergence autistic transgender and non-binary people experience. The aim of this chapter is to frame these experiences outside the predominant neurotypical and cisgender gaze and instead give professionals an opportunity to examine them through a framework inspired by social theories such as those of the performativity of gender and the social model of disability.

The third chapter engages with a discussion around debates concerning autistic transgender and non-binary children and young people, and the main concerns in the process of supporting them. Shain Neumeier uses disability justice and youth liberation frameworks to discuss issues of choice, agency, protection and support as they pertain to younger people and those who may have extensive support needs. They highlight the importance of preserving autonomy and choice in these groups of people, while simultaneously challenging narratives and approaches that encourage paternalism and the dismissal of the children's wishes, by putting the rights of the children themselves in the centre of the discussion.

In the fourth chapter, Reubs Walsh and David Jackson-Perry present some of the theories that 'link' autism and gender variance and challenge the pathologizing attitudes they perpetuate. Instead, they offer alternative theoretical approaches to explain this overlap, which do not rely on considering neurotypicality, abled-bodiedness and cisgenderism to be a norm. In particular, they present the imperfect systems theory, the theory of bottom-up processing, and the flattened priors theory as approaches which may better explain why this overlap between autistic and transgender/non-binary identities may exist. They also discuss some of the challenges autistic transgender and non-binary people may face because they occupy this intersection, such as unintelligibility.

In the fifth chapter, Taylor René Kielsgard and Lydia Brown focus on the intersection of autism, gender variance and race. They present some of the challenges autistic transgender and non-binary people of colour may face, consider the overall concepts of the intersections of autism, neurodivergence, disability, gender variance and race, and make connections in how all of these have interacted in their own lives and in the lives of autistic transgender and non-binary black, Indigenous and people of color (BIPOC) overall. They also present some of the implications of engaging with western concepts around gender variance for people whose cultures do not conceptualize gender in the western, white, and binary way.

Chapters 6, 7 and 8 in Part 2 consist of professional reflections on working with autistic transgender and non-binary people. In Chapter 6, Isabelle Hénault presents the support provided to autistic transgender and non-binary people in gender identity clinics. She includes professional reflections and experiences of supporting autistic transgender and non-binary people in gender identity clinics. She also provides guidelines for helping autistic people to explore their gender identity in ways that distinguish it from sexual orientation, romantic attraction and gender expression, and supplies information on sensory sensitivities such as genital discomfort, and on providing support to them according to their needs. She also provides practical tools that professionals can use to explore these areas with the people they support.

In Chapter 7, Wenn Lawson presents an overview of the areas that some professionals might need to consider when supporting transgender and non-binary autistic people. Specifically, he addresses some of the concerns professionals might have when providing support, the fear of making a mistake and what can be done to address that. He also highlights some of the areas that the professionals might need to explore with the person in order to help them realize what gender identity is right for them, such as interoception, object permanence and sensory differences. He highlights questions around safety as well as how all these may differ between younger and older autistic people.

Chapter 8, written by me and Ella Griffin, focuses on how professionals can develop good relationships with the autistic transgender and non-binary people they are supporting. By exploring examples from the mentor and mentee relationship of the two authors, the chapter gives practical examples of some of the ways in which support might need to be specifically tailored for autistic transgender and non-binary people. We discuss personal biases, documentation and workplace-wide changes as well as suggestions for how to create a supportive relationship in one-to-one sessions. We consider the implications of having these supportive relationships for autistic transgender and non-binary people's safety, security, and agency over their identities.

The third and final part of this book focuses on the embodied and lived experiences of autistic transgender and non-binary people, which may be important to consider for professionals who are supporting them. Chapter 9, written by Alyssa Hillary-Zisk and Jo Minchin, discusses the concepts of interoception and alexithymia. They give an overview of what interoception is, how it is often experienced by autistic people and how it is linked with alexithymia, a difficulty in interpreting and acting on bodily signals. They then go on to elaborate on how interoception and alexithymia may be relevant to the experiences of autistic transgender and non-binary people, using some personal insights.

In Chapter 10, Lexi Orchard discusses the concept of passing and what it might mean for autistic transgender and non-binary people. More importantly, they outline various means which are used to achieve passing, as well as why it might be important. They discuss masking, hiding one's autistic or gender-variant presentations, scripting, adopting behaviours to be perceived as someone other than what the person actually is, and precognition, a process of predicting what the desired outcomes in various situations are and how they might be achieved. This chapter also delves into the implications of what this might mean for a person's overall sense of identity.

In Chapter 11, Olivia Pountney presents the experiences of an autistic transgender woman and discusses various ways in which support was required in various settings, such as education, housing and mental health, as well as by gender identity clinics. She also further presents various strategies that she has adopted in the process of managing the exploration of personal and gender identity, as well as how that has changed over the years. She finally discusses how these experiences may be similar to those of other autistic transgender women, and areas that professionals who support them may need to be aware of.

In the final chapter, Wenn Lawson discusses the experiences of older autistic transgender and non-binary people. He explores some of the reasons that contributed to his realization of his gender much later in life, such as poor interoception, lack of autism awareness and acceptance, receiving various misdiagnoses and having a variety of mental health issues, as well as experiencing professional reluctance to give a gender dysphoria diagnosis to an autistic person. He then discusses a range of implications that this had both on him and his family.

References

American Psychiatric Association (2013) *Diagnostic and Statistical Manual of Mental Disorders* (5th ed.). Arlington, VA: Author.

Baio, J., Wiggins, L., Christensen, D.L., Maenner, M., *et al.* (2018) 'Prevalence of autism spectrum disorder among children aged 8 years – autism and developmental disabilities monitoring network, 11 sites, United States, 2014.' *MMWR Surveillance Summaries*, 67(6), 1–23.

Bargiela, S., Steward, R. & Mandy, W. (2016) 'The experiences of late-diagnosed women with autism spectrum conditions: An investigation of the female autism phenotype.' *Journal of Autism and Developmental Disorders*, 46(10), 3281–3294.

Baron-Cohen, S. & J. Hammer, J. (1997) 'Is autism an extreme form of the "male brain"?' *Advances in Infancy Research*, 11: 193–218.

BBC News (2020) 'Puberty blockers: Under-16s "unlikely to be able to give informed consent".' Available at: www.bbc.co.uk/news/uk-england-cambridgeshire-55144148 [accessed 27 February 2021].

Brown, X.Z., L. (2011) 'The significance of semantics: Person-first language: Why it matters.' Autistichoya.com. Available at: www.autistichoya.com/2011/08/significance-of-semantics-person-first.html [accessed 27 February 2021].

Connolly, M.D., Zervos, M.J., Barone II, C.J., Johnson, C.C. & Joseph, C.L. (2016) 'The mental health of transgender youth: Advances in understanding.' *Journal of Adolescent Health*, 59(5), 489–495.

Davidson, J. & Tamas, S. (2016) 'Autism and the ghost of gender.' *Emotion, Space and Society*, 19: 59–65.

Delphy, C. (1993) 'Rethinking sex and gender.' *Women's Studies International Forum*, 16(1), 1–9.

Dworzynski, K., Ronald, A., Bolton, P. & Happé, F. (2012) 'How different are girls and boys above and below the diagnostic threshold for autism spectrum disorders?' *Journal of the American Academy of Child & Adolescent Psychiatry*, 51(8), 788–797.

Fausto-Sterling, A. (2012) *Sex/Gender: Biology in a Social World*. New York, NY: Routledge.

George, R. & Stokes, M.A. (2017) 'Gender identity and sexual orientation in autism spectrum disorder.' *Autism*, 0(0), 1–13.

Halladay, A.K., Bishop, S., Constantino, J.N., Daniels, A.M. *et al.* (2015) 'Sex and gender differences in autism spectrum disorder: Summarizing evidence gaps and identifying emerging areas of priority.' *Molecular Autism*, 6(1), 1–5.

Kenny, L., Hattersley, C., Molins, B., Buckley, C., Povey, C. & Pellicano, E. (2016) 'Which terms should be used to describe autism? Perspectives from the UK autism community.' *Autism*, 20(4), 442–462.

Kourti, M. & MacLeod, A. (2019) '"I don't feel like a gender, I feel like myself": Autistic individuals raised as girls exploring gender identity.' *Autism in Adulthood*, 1(1), 52–59.

Matson, J.L. & Kozlowski, A.M. (2011) 'The increasing prevalence of autism spectrum disorders.' *Research in Autism Spectrum Disorders*, 5(1), 418–425.

Milton, D.E. (2012) 'On the ontological status of autism: The "double empathy problem".' *Disability & Society*, 27(6), 883–887.

Murray, D., Lesser, M. & Lawson, W. (2005). Attention, monotropism and the diagnostic criteria for autism. Autism, 9(2), 139-156.

Oakley, A. (1972/1985) *Sex, Gender and Society*. London: Temple Smith (revised edition, 1985, Gower).

Rice, C.E., Rosanoff, M., Dawson, G. & Durkin, M.S. *et al.* (2012) 'Evaluating changes in the prevalence of the autism spectrum disorders (ASDs).' *Public Health Reviews*, 34(2), 1–22.

Rivet, T.T. & Matson, J.L. (2011) 'Review of gender differences in core symptomatology in autism spectrum disorders.' *Research in Autism Spectrum Disorders*, 5(3), 957–976.

Sinclair, J. (2013) 'Why I dislike "person first" language.' *Autonomy, the Critical Journal of Interdisciplinary Autism Studies*, 1(2), 2–3.

Singer, J. (1999) 'Why can't you be normal for once in your life? From a "Problem with no Name" to a new category of disability.' In M. Corker & S. French (eds), *Disability Discourse* (pp.59–67). Buckingham/Philadelphia: Open University Press.

Werling, D.M. & Geschwind, D.H. (2013) 'Sex differences in autism spectrum disorders.' *Current Opinion in Neurology*, 26(2), 146.

Wilkinson, L.A. (2008) 'The gender gap in Asperger Syndrome: Where are the girls?' *Teaching Exceptional Children Plus*, 4(4), n4.

Chapter 2

'Here Comes Trouble'

AUTISM AND GENDER PERFORMANCE

Damian E.M. Milton

Introduction

When one thinks of gender identity and its formation, there has long been a tense discussion between those who see gendered behaviour as highly dependent on one's biological makeup and those who would see gender as primarily a social identity. The first approach has had a significant impact on how conceptualizations of autism have developed, with autism traditionally seen as a 'disorder' impacting on young males at a far higher rate than females. This tradition has, however, led to a cultural bias in diagnostic practice, with many people perceived to be women not being referred for assessment. In parallel to this development has been critique of such a biologically 'essentialist' approach to gender from feminist scholars such as Judith Butler (1990, 1993). In this chapter, the theories of Butler and those of sociologist Erving Goffman (1959, 1963) are drawn on to explore how gender is 'performed' in a social context and how the performances of gendered identities of autistic people can be seen as subversive of traditional social expectations.

One of the ways in which people are identified as autistic is in their non-conformity to societal expectations, with social performance more generally being conceptualized as disordered and deficient. This narrative of what it is to be autistic can be particularly impactful when fused with social expectations of gender identity and performance, on how others perceive you and how you develop a sense of selfhood. It is suggested in this chapter that autistic ways of being naturally subvert gendered norms and expectations. However, this can come with personal costs to the autistic person. Concepts covered in this chapter include shifting conceptualizations of autism, masking, and 'gender policing' through the enforcement of social sanctions for performances of gender deemed 'deviant'.

Gender identity is highly significant for professionals working with autistic people, whether openly (and knowingly) gender variant or not. This chapter aims to give a clear account of the relevance of the concept of gender performance to professionals working with autistic people and their loved ones. It is hoped that it will also be of use to those autistic people reading this book who wish to reflect on the intersection between being autistic and gender identity.

Shifting conceptualizations of autism

Traditionally, academic accounts have positioned autism as a biological and psychological deviance from expected norms of childhood development. In more recent times, however, such conceptualizations have come under scrutiny by proponents of the neurodiversity paradigm (Milton, 2017), often exploring experiences of autism through a social model of disability. Within such a conceptualization, autism can be seen as a way of being in the world that is often discriminated against in society. This is not to diminish the impact of what may be described as the effects of embodied differences or the effects of impairment, but to see autistic lives as socially situated. Among the proponents of this have been autistic scholars who have proposed alternative theories for understanding autistic experiences. These theories have tended to receive less attention than more dominant theories of autism such as executive dysfunction or theory of mind, yet they offer much in regard to understanding autistic identity formation.

An interest model of autism

Also termed 'monotropism', this model of autism originated in the work of Dinah Murray (Murray, 1992; Murray, Lesser & Lawson, 2005) and influenced the work of Wenn Lawson (2010). The starting point for this theory is that perceptual attention is seen as a scarce resource, with autistic people tending towards a 'monotropic' (based on highly focused interests) rather than 'polytropic' (broad) attentional style. The shifting of attention, use of language and social interaction are all tasks that need a broad attention (Murray *et al.*, 2005), but could become difficult for those with a more monotropic use of attention – i.e. autistic people. Such an account highlights how autistic people often develop passionate interests that are sustained over long periods of time, and yet there are also downsides, such as the distress caused by interruptions to their attention. 'We suggest that the uneven skills profile in autism depends on which interests have been fired into monotropic super drive and which have been left unstimulated by any felt experience (Murray *et al.*, 2005, p.143).

The double empathy problem

Using the accounts of autistic people as a foundation, Milton (2012) suggested that rather than seeing social interaction difficulties as solely located within the mind of the autistic person, the social disjuncture felt by autistic people is often mirrored by those attempting to understand and interact with them. In this sense, it is both parties that can struggle to empathize with the other. Since its inception, the theory has been supported by numerous experimental research studies (Milton, Heasman & Sheppard, 2018).

Utilizing an interest model of autism and the concept of the double empathy problem not only reframes what has been understood as dysfunctional and restricted interests and social behaviours, but gives autistic people, their families and those working with them ways in which to understand development and identity without doing so purely in terms of deficit and disorder.

The performance of gendered identities

No doubt influenced by the work of William Shakespeare, Goffman (1959) argued that the social identities that people create through their interactions could be likened to actors on a stage, with what is referred to as the 'dramaturgical analogy'. Social actors put on various 'masks' and doubt the existence of an authentic 'real self' behind the various masks that people put on in order to interact with others. Similarly, Butler (1990, 1993) argued that the reality of gender only existed through how it was enacted and performed by people in their social interactions. For Butler, there was no self as such that precedes a gendered 'self'. From the moment we are born, we are subjected to the gendered expectations of others. In this sense, gender is seen as constructed through the stylized repetitive performance of gendered acts, an imitation or mime of dominant conventions. A performance rather than an expression.

The idea that there is no such thing as a pre-linguistic self-identity is debatable, however (Milton, 2017), especially when one considers the ways of being of so-called 'non-verbal' autistic people. Also, whether one is fully aware of what gender refers to or not, one will have gendered expectations placed on one. What these theories do highlight, however, is how autistic ways of being are often unlikely to match with social expectations of the performance of gender.

Autistic people are often said to have difficulties in mimicking others. How would autistic people identify and perform gender? Or do so with a mismatch of salient interests (Milton, 2017) to refer to regarding their performance of gender identity? Simply by being autistic, an individual may be subverting gendered expectations, developing idiosyncratically in what has been termed by some as 'neuroqueer' (Yergeau, 2018). As Butler (1990, p.135) wrote, 'The construction of coherence conceals the gender discontinuities that run rampant.'

The social context of the interaction between autistic and gendered identities is likely to be one of incongruence. This feeling of incongruence can have a myriad of consequences, but it is likely to impact on feelings of selfhood and social belonging. Having a body that does not perform to gendered social expectations, or does so at potentially great personal cost from 'masking', creates a dissonance that needs to be psychologically resolved in some way or may have a continued negative impact on someone's well-being.

The narrow constraints by which gender norms are often formed will produce a barrier for many autistic people. They may be inaccessible to follow, they may appear at odds with how one views oneself, or one may try to follow them closely, still to be judged to have failed.

An interesting facet of gender performance is the need for effort (or indeed labour) in order to maintain it. Many features of performing femininity require much effort (e.g. the use of makeup), while the performance of masculinity requires a lack of it (e.g. being viewed as somewhat unkempt is comparatively less stigmatized).

Gender policing

Subverting gendered social expectations does come with associated costs in the form of social sanctions and discrimination. One can see many similarities between the 'policing' of the 'misbehaviour' of both autistic and gender-variant people. Indeed, given the above theories, it could be expected that there would be a high crossover between the two. According to Butler, if gendered self-identifications are not cultivated and lack coherence, or indeed are 'hyper-cultivated', this will mark someone out from the norm, leading to social sanction and shaming. In this sense, one does not make a social identification on the basis of a given anatomy alone, but one cultivates such an identity over time in a context of the gender 'policing' from others.

A 'hyper-cultivated' gender performance, although certainly not universal, can be one way in which autistic people may even attempt to mask being autistic, or else be the manifestation of an incongruent sense of self. Indeed, internalizing such gender roles, especially to extremes, can become highly toxic. Goffman (1963) regarded social stigma as the disjuncture between the way someone acts, and the way others would wish them to. He talked about how one managed social interaction if one carried a visible or invisible 'spoiled identity'. Not only do autistic people carry stigmatized 'spoiled' social identities, but we may also struggle to manage social interactions (though this may be partly because of this stigma and othering). In this sense, we all 'police' our own gender performance and that of others according to Butler's theory (although this presumes a 'self-awareness' that is constructed in a social context). However, masking can bring with it serious repercussions in terms of exhaustion, stress, and damage to selfhood, and has been linked to mental health difficulties in autistic people. A further discussion on masking can also be found in Chapter 10.

Key for the enforcement of gender roles for Butler (1993) is the ideology of heterosexuality, an 'idealization' of gender roles and sexuality that is never fully achievable in practice, as there would be no need to define a heterosexual norm without there being something outside its boundaries to be considered socially taboo. Transgressions of heteronormativity such as LGBTQ+ (lesbian, gay, bisexual, transgender and queer or questioning and others) subcultures fall within culture, yet can be said to be outside the dominant culture.

Subversion

When Butler (1990, p.138) says, 'parodic proliferation deprives hegemonic culture and its critics of the claim to naturalized or essentialist gender identities', she is suggesting that the dominance of this ideology is disrupted by the parodying of gender roles and identities. From this perspective, Butler suggests that drag acts carry a subversive power, challenging established meanings through both reflecting and imitating dominant gender performance, while disputing the claim that it is in any way the only and 'natural' way to perform social acts. Gender is thus exposed as a simulation, a copy, a performance where idealization is never truly achievable. For Butler, subverting gender identity is neither an easy task nor one that can be made by choice as such, and certainly not a consumer style someone can 'buy in' to. For Butler, to be subversive one must both mimic and displace established conventions.

If it is the case that subversive acts require both the miming of dominant norms and the displacing of them, are the enactments of autistic people by their very social dispositions 'subversive' in their displacement of norms, as once described as 'nature's answer to over-conformity' (Milton, 2017)? Does the presence of autistic people confound fantasies of selfhood and gender to the extent of attracting the social sanctioning of others? One could also say, however, that along with the sanctions and harms of autistic gender performance comes a subversive power in the disposition of the 'neuroqueer' (Yergeau, 2018) to challenge the need for such strict boundaries for social roles and expectations.

Implications for practice

For those working with autistic people, the above outlined theories pose a problem for practice. There is a significant tension between the role of a teacher (as an example) in terms of helping an individual develop new skills and 'fit in' to society, and what is salient to the autistic person they are working with. This is particularly pertinent to gender identity. A practitioner who enforces gendered expectations may be setting an autistic person up for failure or exhaustion and burnout from social 'masking'. Some examples of explorations of gender-variant expressions in autistic people by professionals working in gender identity clinics can be found in Chapter 6. The development of autistic-led autism theory, such as an interest model or the double empathy problem, show that autistic performances of gender are likely to be idiosyncratic, even potentially subversive, and their suppression highly damaging to selfhood and self-esteem.

A key message when working with any autistic person is not to see their 'autism' as something separate to them and their identity to be rectified or remedied in some way, but as a way of being to be respected and worked with. This may include performances of gender that one might find 'challenging', but ultimately rewarding given the space to be so. It also may include other aspects of their identity, such as race, as discussed in Chapter 5. If professionals wish to help autistic people make their own sense of gender identity, they must give them the space and support to explore it. In order to build a congruent sense of self, acceptance of autistic ways of being needs to extend to gender performance. This may mean placing one's own beliefs about gender to one side.

A theory and method that I have personally found useful through numerous projects is personal construct theory (PCT), developed in the 1950s by George Kelly (1970). The starting point for this theory is how people idiosyncratically make sense of the world and construct meaning from it. Working with these constructs rather than imposing them onto autistic people is a good starting point for professionals to consider. This requires rapport and respect in interactions, and is not possible if the autistic person they are working with continues to feel that they are being judged negatively for the way they think or act.

References

Butler, J. (1990) *Gender Trouble*. London: Routledge.

Butler, J. (1993) *Bodies That Matter*. London: Routledge.

Goffman, E. (1959) *The Presentation of Self in Everyday Life*. Harmondsworth: Penguin.

Goffman, E. (1963) *Stigma: Notes on the Management of a Spoiled Identity*. Harmondsworth: Penguin.

Kelly, G.A. (1970) 'A brief introduction to personal construct theory.' *Perspectives in Personal Construct Theory*, 1, 29.

Lawson, W. (2010) *The Passionate Mind: How People with Autism Learn*. London: Jessica Kingsley Publishers.

Milton, D. (2012) 'On the ontological status of autism: The "double empathy problem".' *Disability and Society*, 27(6), 883–887.

Milton, D. (2017) *A Mismatch of Salience: Explorations in Autism from Theory to Practice*. Hove: Pavilion.

Milton, D., Heasman, B. & Sheppard, E. (2018). 'Double Empathy.' In F. Volkmar (ed.), *Encyclopaedia of Autism Spectrum Disorders*. New York, NY: Springer.

Murray, D. (1992) 'Attention Tunnelling and Autism.' In P. Shattock & G. Linfoot (eds), *Living with Autism: The Individual, the Family and the Professional*. Durham Research Conference, April 1995, pp.83–193.

Murray, D., Lesser, M. & Lawson, W. (2005) 'Attention, monotropism and the diagnostic criteria for autism.' *Autism*, 9(2), 136–156.

Yergeau, M. (2018) *Authoring Autism: On Rhetoric and Neurological Queerness*. Durham, NC: Duke University Press.

Chapter 3

Beyond 'For Your Own Good'

YOUTH LIBERATION, DISABILITY JUSTICE AND THE IMPORTANCE OF AUTONOMY IN THE LIVES OF AUTISTIC TRANSGENDER CHILDREN

Shain M. Neumeier

Introduction

The most common response I get from other adults in advocating for youth rights and liberation is, 'But have you ever been a parent?' To which I answer, 'No, but I remember what it was like to be a child too well not to support other children's self-determination.'

Similarly, neurotypical parents' go-to rebuttal to my arguments for the rights of other autistic people is, 'You're not like my autistic child!' My response to this is that I have been and still am more like their autistic children than they think, and more so than they, as neurotypical people, will ever be.

Here, then, lies the difficulty of writing about the needs of transgender autistic children: at the time I was one, I did not know it. Neither autism nor gender identity had entered the mainstream cultural discussion to any meaningful degree at the time. Instead, the general consensus on this only sporadically gender-conforming child with countless texture and sound aversions, a preference for animals over most people, and a personality frequently described as 'intense', as well as several other visible and invisible disabilities, was that they were just 'weird, not otherwise specified'. Therefore, for better and for worse in various ways, transgender autistic children's experiences are very different in today's climate than they were in the 1990s.

What I do know a lot about, though, is autonomy: why it is important, the effects of denying it to people, and how people nonetheless justify denying it. Put together, my experiences and those of other people who grew up autistic and transgender have led to the conclusion that what we choose for ourselves will never be as bad as the things other people force on us 'for our own good'.

The problems with paternalism

It is difficult to talk about the experiences, perspectives and needs of autistic transgender children as a totally separate set of issues from those affecting neurotypical transgender children, cisgender autistic children, or transgender autistic adults (especially those under guardianship or institutionalized care). The problem facing all of them is paternalism – the belief that other people, namely neurotypical, cisgender adults, know what is best for them better than they do, and thus that these other people should be able to make decisions for them, down to the most basic and fundamental aspects of life.

According to this belief, childhood or disability (including, in the minds of some people, the so-called mental illness of gender variance) is proof of someone's inability to make any major decisions about their life all on their own. Because the person cannot (yet) be as independent as the average adult is (expected to be), individual authority figures, institutions, and the culture at large disempower them in all areas without taking into account what they might be capable of, especially when they have the right kinds of support. It is essentially the idea of 'my house, my rules', but on a larger scale – support comes at the cost of autonomy.

Built into the idea of paternalism is the assumption that parents, guardians and other caregivers make better decisions than a child or person with a disability would make for themselves, and always with that person's best interests in mind. Even if caregivers did always have good intentions, this would not necessarily mean that their decisions would be better than those of the people most directly affected by them. A lot of the time, caregivers make decisions about the lives of those they have power over based on what they themselves (think they) would want, or what they think the other person should want based on their own worldviews, at the expense of the actual person's needs and preferences.

On top of this – and only partially because of it – is the concept of parental rights, which entitles parents to treat their children more or less how they want based on their own preferences and beliefs (Troxel v. Granville, 2000).[1] This is the only present-day context in the United States where a civil right exists to give one group of people power over other human beings (Godwin, 2015).[2] Among other problems, it has created a situation in which the law allows parents to intentionally hurt children in the name of 'discipline', in a way that would never be acceptable (at least on paper) against a person's spouse, or for that matter their parents. Even short of that, it allows parents to impose their own prejudices and expectations on their children based on the unspoken belief that parents deserve to have the child they want, even if it comes at the expense of the child they have.

A prime example of the harmful ways in which all of this plays out in the lives of autistic, transgender and otherwise disabled or queer children is coercive and abusive youth behaviour modification programmes. Among others, these include two forms that are historically linked: applied behaviour analysis (ABA), and so-called conversion or reparative therapy.

While current supporters and providers say that the goal of ABA is to teach autistic children new skills, the original intent behind it was to make them indistinguishable from their peers through operant behavioural conditioning (Devita-Raeburn, 2016; The Lovaas Centre, 1987). In the past, ABA openly relied on inflicting extreme forms of punishment on autistic children, including the use of cattle prods

---

1 'The liberty interest at issue in this case – the interest of parents in the care, custody, and control of their children – is perhaps the oldest of the fundamental liberty interests recognized by this Court.'

2 American jurisprudence around the concept of parental rights amounts to establishing that parents have a quasi-property interest in their children.

(Brown, n.d.).[3] ABA apologists today are quick to point out that this is no longer the case. Even so, so-called 'positive interventions' can be functionally aversive in practice, limiting an autistic child's access to preferred communication styles and sources of comfort until they comply with a therapist's demands, even when those demands involve severe discomfort such as forced eye contact and exposure to sensory aversions (*Life Magazine*, 1965).

Similarly, conversion or reparative therapy aims to force LGBTQ+ youth to become, or at least pretend to be, heterosexual and gender conforming (The Trevor Project, n.d.). As with ABA, so-called treatment has included the use of painful aversive interventions like electric shock as well as seemingly innocuous approaches such as talk therapy (Bothe, 2020).

Both of these practices trace back in significant part to the work of Ole Ivar Lovaas, a researcher and behaviourist at the University of California, Los Angeles, during the 1960s and 1970s. As an assistant professor, he began a programme of treatment that would evolve into ABA, which he described as 'holding any mentally crippled child accountable for his behaviour and...forcing him to act normal'(*Life Magazine*, 1965). Later, in collaboration with conversion therapy proponent George Rekers, he conducted a series of studies on the use of behaviour modification on gender-variant children (Rekers & Lovaas, 1974; Rekers, Lovaas & Low, 1974; Rekers *et al.*, 1977; Rekers *et al.*, 1978). The most infamous of these experiments involved having a couple reward their four-year-old son for stereotypically masculine behaviours and physically punish him for stereotypically feminine behaviours (Rekers & Lovaas, 1974). The subject of this study grew up to be a gay man, but ultimately died by suicide, which his family came to believe was a result of their participation in the study (Bronstein & Joseph, 2011).

This man was far from the only victim of conversion therapy, let alone other forms of behavioural modification used on children with their parents' consent, allegedly for their own good. Many survivors

---

3   At least one facility, the Judge Rotenberg Educational Center, continues to openly use electric shock, food deprivation and restraint on neurodivergent people as part of its behaviour modification programme.

of these methods and programmes have written about the trauma they experienced and its later effects, including but not limited to how such coercive techniques essentially groomed them for further abuse (e.g. Bascom, 2011; Fox, 2015; Jones, 2013). Nonetheless, parents can still legally force their children to undergo conversion therapy in the majority of US states, despite the growing recognition that it is harmful and ineffective (The Trevor Project, n.d.).[4] ABA, meanwhile, is not only legal across the country and in various countries all over the world, but remains the most common treatment for autism (Devita-Raeburn, 2016).

In these and other cases, the harms resulting from paternalism can be as bad as those caused by outright malice or hatred. Arguably, they are worse. After all, the argument that coercion and pain can be for someone's own good provides cover for practices that would otherwise be clearly abusive and for any underlying selfish motivations. Furthermore, the betrayal involved in someone's alleged loved ones intentionally hurting them or allowing others to do so is profoundly traumatic all on its own. It damages both a person's ability to trust others and their sense of self-worth to know that their own family would rather have them suffer than accept them as they are. As a result, it can set a person up for future abuse based on the association between love and pain; the belief that they cannot expect better; the belief that they deserve to be hurt; or some combination of the three.

A youth liberation and disability justice approach

But what is the alternative? Questioning paternalism in the lives of children and disabled people, and especially disabled children, inevitably leads to hypothetical questions about touching hot stoves, running into traffic, or refusing treatment in a medical emergency, with the assumption being that a youth liberationist or disability justice advocate would oppose any kind of intervention.

Neither youth liberation nor disability justice requires such a

---

4   Conversion therapy remains legal in 30 states in the United States.

position, though. Instead, here are two of the core beliefs of both youth liberationists and disability justice advocates:

1. Children and disabled people are full people in their own right, with rights and interests distinct from but equally valid as those of their parents and other caregivers.

2. A person's need for support does not make them less capable of exercising autonomy or less deserving of it.

Youth liberationists and disability justice advocates also recognize that current conditions make the full implications of these beliefs impractical, if not impossible. However, as long as current laws, institutions and customs disempower children and disabled people, non-disabled adults must recognize the extent of the power they have and use it in accordance with these principles to the extent possible. This includes affirmatively using this power to protect the people in their care against the by-products of ageism and ableism, such as peer abuse in schools and treatment facilities, when refusing to take a stand would send the message to all involved that some people are fair game for abuse. Alternatively, it also requires that parents and caregivers refuse to use their power to force children or disabled people to be normal and obedient for their own sake, even in the face of outside pressure.

Under this framework, therefore, parents and caregivers would not only have the right to pull a child's hand away from a hot stove or push a disabled adult out of the way of a moving truck; they would have an obligation to do so. What it does not allow is for punishment, or for broad restrictions based on a possible risk, more than a friend or spouse could impose on a rescued loved one. Furthermore, the parent or caregiver has the responsibility to support the person without coercion or pain in learning the skills that will allow them to exercise their autonomy safely, within that person's boundaries and using a communication style accessible to them.

Where the full extent of autonomy is not possible, such as in the case of a five-year-old giving or refusing consent for chemotherapy, the person in question should nonetheless have as much control over their situation as possible, including talking to the person about what's happening and why, and giving people choices about the process (for instance, which arm to receive an injection in) that will make it more tolerable. Most importantly, parents, guardians, doctors, therapists and educators must never lose sight of the fact that they are dealing with a full person who experiences pain, remembers traumatic events, and overall has an independent perspective regardless of their decision-making abilities.

Not every situation is as drastic as the hypothetical scenarios that people always seem to raise immediately. Most will not be. Therefore, in most cases, broad categorical restrictions are not justifiable, and it is crucial for parents and caregivers to keep in mind the distinction between what the person they're responsible for is and what they want that person to be, between what that person needs and what they want for that person. One of the most crucial tasks for a parent or caregiver is to support and enable a child or disabled person to lead the life that that person finds fulfilling, knowing that they, more than anyone else, will have to live with the consequences of the decisions made about them.

Paternalism, pathologization and the dialogue around autistic and transgender children

Unfortunately, we are nowhere near a society that works from youth liberationist or disability justice principles. Instead, the presumption that children (and particularly autistic children) are incapable of making major decisions about their lives or even understanding themselves, and the belief that they are extensions, or even quasi-property, of their parents, have made them talking points for transphobic ideas and practices.

The rhetoric of the backlash against increased recognition of gender-variant people is essentially the bastard lovechild of the myths of the autism epidemic and the homosexual agenda. Transphobic culture warriors have made the same mistake as the autism fearmongers by taking increased visibility as proof of a new phenomenon (and, in this case, as wider acceptance than actually exists).

Meanwhile, both cultural conservatives and some self-described feminists have transparently repackaged the same beliefs that were once common about gay, lesbian and bisexual people, only this time casting transgender people in the role of sexual predators trying to lure children into a deviant lifestyle. One aspect of this narrative is the overblown if not totally imaginary fears that transgender women in particular (or, as they see it, men pretending to be transgender women) will harass and even sexually assault cisgender girls and women if allowed access to women-only spaces. The risks of these attitudes to autistic transgender people who may need access to those spaces are further discussed in Chapter 11. A second aspect that is infuriatingly condescending, if somewhat less overtly stigmatizing, is the argument that transgender adults and our allies have preyed on or outright stoked the internalized misogyny of gender non-conforming girls to convince them to identify as men, as opposed to tomboys or butch lesbians.

People who oppose recognizing and respecting gender-variant children's identities emphasize, if not intentionally exaggerate, the number of children who turn out to be cisgender after all, while necessarily downplaying the harms of even supposedly well-meaning transphobia. Their arguments on these points have several flaws. First of all, their positions are not supported by the research (e.g. Brooks, 2018; Sorbara, 2020; World Professional Association for Transgender Health, 2011).[5] They also incorrectly assume that it is worse to support someone in a choice that that person will later come to regret than it is to deny that person's ability to make a decision in the first place.

Most significantly, though, they assume that recognizing gender-variant children's identities will inevitably and automatically result in permanent medical transition, including hormone replacement therapy and gender-confirmation surgery. In doing so, they ignore that not every transgender person experiences bodily dysphoria, and that not all transgender people who do experience it can or want to

---

5   'Older age and later pubertal stage at the time of presentation to [gender-affirm-
     ing medical care] are associated with increased rates of psychoactive medication
     use and increased rates of mental health problems (depression and anxiety),
     respectively' (Sorbara *et al.* 2020, p.7).

undergo medical transition. It also reveals an ignorance of what the existing standards of care and practices among transgender health-care providers actually are.

The World Professional Association for Transgender Health's standards of care (2011), for instance, include explicit criteria for providing reversible, partially reversible and irreversible forms of gender-affirming medical treatment to children and adolescents. Instead, the fearmongers choose to misrepresent the relatively recent changes to the standards of care that reduce the amount of gatekeeping imposed on the transgender population as a whole as evidence that treatment professionals are hastily and carelessly putting children through irreversible medical procedures (e.g. Rowling, 2020). To the extent that social transition options such as wearing clothing or using facilities that match the child's gender identity enter into the discussion at all, it's only to frame transgender youth themselves as dangerous to their cisgender peers.

All of this undermines the common deflection from accusations of transphobia, that the people making these arguments have nothing against actual transgender people and are simply concerned about the dangers of imposing an ideology or agenda on children and society at large. In reality, the only things they have to back up their argument that adults are imposing their own political agendas on gender non-conforming children are speculation and scattered stories of people transitioning back to their assigned gender at birth.

The shrill fearmongering and condescending paternalism only increases when applied to autistic children.[6] A variety of public figures ranging from Harry Potter author J.K. Rowling to disgraced right-wing troll Milo Yiannopoulos have attempted to justify their transphobia by claiming that autistic children, and particularly autistic girls, are being misled into identifying as transgender. The unspoken assumption behind this talking point is that autistic children – especially those they consider to be girls – are uniquely incapable of understanding the concept of gender and their relationship to it.

---

6   It's telling how no one I've run across making this argument has ever been involved in efforts to address the actual problems facing autistic children, such as restraint and seclusion in schools or forced participation in ABA programmes.

This talking point matches up in part with views expressed by Simon Baron-Cohen (2010), who certain neurotypicals generally consider an expert on autism, and who has actually done research on the overlap between the autistic and transgender communities. Among the reasons that many autistic people don't share this confidence in his understanding of our community is his theory that autistic people are inherently systemizing rather than empathizing, and that we therefore have 'extreme male brains' (Markram & Markram, 2010).[7] In discussing the overlap between the autistic and transgender communities, Baron-Cohen and other researchers have pointed to this theory as an explanation for why autistic people assigned female at birth may be transmasculine (Jones *et al.*, 2011). The 'extreme male brain' theory does not explain the existence of transfeminine autistic people, to say nothing of those of us who are non-binary.

Still other people have sought to de-legitimize young autistic people's gender identities by framing them as 'obsessions' about gender, as if the autistic tendency to learn everything about a topic would make us less able to understand it well enough to accurately apply it to our own lives (e.g. Strang *et al.*, 2018).

Better explanations for the connection between autism and gender variance

It is very likely that the large crossover between the autistic and transgender communities is more than a coincidence, and that autism does have a significant impact on how we understand gender and its role in our lives. Several studies have found a significant correlation between autism and gender variance (e.g. de Vries *et al.*, 2010; Warrier *et al.*, 2020). It is not, however, because autistic people are especially suggestible or that we easily succumb to peer pressure. If anything, we're less motivated by other people's perceptions and approval of

---

7 One alternative explanation is that autistic people actually experience emotions and other stimuli more intensely than neurotypical people, and that the cognitive style that Baron-Cohen classifies as 'systemizing' is an attempt to cope with what would otherwise be overwhelming.

us than neurotypicals are (Hu *et al.*, 2021).[8] Even if we were more susceptible to social pressure than average, the pressure adults and peers alike put on autistic children to be 'normal' makes it highly unlikely that any significant amount of people are pressuring them into identifying as transgender. It certainly has nothing to do with any false dichotomy between allegedly masculine systemizing brains and supposedly feminine empathizing ones.

Instead, because autistic people are less likely to see neurotypical social norms as inherently valuable even after we become aware of them, it is unsurprising that we would be less invested in upholding or conforming to gender roles. After all, they are essentially arbitrary clusters of personality traits, interests, appearances and social roles assigned to people based on body parts and functions that don't even universally line up into the two categories that neurotypical society chooses to recognize as valid, as it has already been discussed in Chapter 2. There is no concrete and indisputable reason why we can't or shouldn't be able to identify with the category that we see ourselves in the most, or even with one we custom-create, and live authentically according to that self-understanding.

Additionally, we have fewer barriers to coming out to ourselves and others, where few if any of us will have spent any significant amount of time being able to imagine we are normal. This is especially the case for autistic children, who cannot escape peers and adult authority figures reminding them they are not what they're supposed to be and thus don't belong. In many cases, therefore, the risks to autistic people's self-esteem and reputations in recognizing and admitting that we are outliers in yet another way are fewer than they might otherwise have been.

Without a strong need to fit in to our assigned gender roles for our own sake, we are more likely to factor other things that more immediately affect our well-being into how we express our gender, if not how we define it. These may include other aspects of our autistic

---

8   'The results showed that while healthy controls were more likely to make the moral choice when they were observed in the Public condition (vs. Private[...]), ASD patients did not change their behaviors significantly depending on the presence or absence of a witness' (Hu *et al.*, 2021).

neurology, such as wearing or avoiding certain gendered clothes for sensory reasons or engaging in gendered activities that relate to our areas of special interest. By themselves, such factors, many of which are further explored in Chapter 4, would not make us (identify as) transgender, but they may have some influence on how we relate to gender, and how we choose to transition, if at all.

All of this may or may not apply to any transgender or gender non-conforming autistic child. Either way, it does not make the child's gender identity any more or less valid than that of a neuro-typical child, or a transgender autistic adult.

Conclusion: being an ally to transgender autistic children

The extent of ageism, ableism and transphobia, and of the harms they can cause, makes it essential that adults support autistic transgender children as much as possible. Here are some ways that educators, healthcare providers and other professionals can do so:

1. Focus on the child in front of you. Autistic transgender children are not pawns or talking points. They are not incomplete people to be moulded into what the adults around them want them to be. They are at least as sensitive to pain and discomfort – including rejection, invalidation, bullying and gender dysphoria – as neurotypical children, and quite likely more so, and will therefore be strongly affected by decisions others make on their behalf, for better and for worse. Adults must take this into account by deliberately setting aside their own biases in goals in favour of learning what the gender-variant autistic children in their lives individually want, what they need to attain it, and how they can be supported in clarifying and accessing it to the fullest extent possible. More information about how to build good relationships with autistic gender-variant people can be found in Chapter 8.

2. Provide autistic transgender children with knowledge and language to help them understand their identities. Labels are not inherently bad or limiting, and in fact they can be crucial to a

person's ability to understand themselves. As it is, autistic and transgender children already receive many harmful messages about their value and place in the world. Having access to alternative ways of seeing themselves, as well as judgement-free opportunities to discuss, clarify and make decisions based on an affirming self-concept, is therefore crucial to the well-being of a child belonging to both communities.

3. Put the child (and yourself) in contact with autistic transgender adults. For such a relatively small community, we are very easy to find, especially, though not exclusively, online. Furthermore, we generally want to protect the next generation of people like us from going through the same problems we experienced. Many of us are therefore more than willing to be mentors to younger gender-variant autistic people and resources for teachers and healthcare providers who want to better understand the perspectives of the children in their care.

4. Offer to advocate on the child's behalf in talking with other school officials and treatment providers, without forcing the child to accept help they do not want. In particular, respect the child's decisions about privacy regarding their gender identity, autism diagnosis, or both. More generally, when offering help, be very explicit and open in asking about the child's boundaries and take the time to come up with creative ways to support them within these parameters.

5. Identify and provide accommodations that will make the transition process as accessible as possible. Autistic people often have specific access needs around things such as communication and sensory input, which are further discussed in Chapter 7. This may require providing plain-language, concrete explanations of concepts and procedures, and even communication devices that will allow them to fully participate in discussions around transition. It may also involve altering how medical care is provided to accommodate a child's sensory aversions, such as setting explicit boundaries around how and when

a provider can touch the child's body, to minimize sensory discomfort or trauma. Furthermore, autistic people frequently have other physical and mental health conditions that may need to be accounted for in the transition process, especially, but not exclusively, in the medical context. Because of the significant overlap between the autistic and transgender communities, doctors and therapists providing gender-affirming care to children should be proactive in recognizing the need for, and proposing, potential accommodations in working with their patients, even when they do not have an official autism diagnosis.

6. Validate an autistic child's gender identity even while allowing for the possibility that they may identify differently in the future. It is possible that a given autistic person may later decide to transition back to the gender assigned to them at birth, but it's better to allow them the dignity of risk than to force them to live inauthentically because they might later want to make a different choice. Puberty is as hard to reverse as medical transition, and hormone blockers can postpone the need to make a more permanent decision either way. If nothing else, validating and respecting the child from the start will build trust, and therefore make it more likely that they will take any concerns you have about transition-related issues seriously later on.

Always, always, ALWAYS have the child's back. Both autistic children and transgender children have plenty of reasons to feel as if it is them against the world. This is even more the case for children living at the intersection of these identities. Whether an autistic transgender person emerges from their childhood as a well-adjusted adult depends heavily on whether they feel that the adults in their lives, including teachers and healthcare providers as well as parents, acted the part. If not, it will be difficult for them to trust other people, or to believe that they are worth anyone's support. They will inevitably learn how harsh the 'real world' can be to people who are different if they have not already; it does not need to come from you. If instead you are there to show the autistic transgender child in your life that others can choose to be kind and that they deserve kindness, they'll be better prepared to hold up under the hardships they're likely to face

References

Baron-Cohen, S. (2010) 'Empathizing, systemizing, and the extreme male brain theory of autism.' *Progress in Brain Research*, 186: 167–175.

Bascom, J. (2011, 5 October) 'Quiet hands.' Available at https://juststimming.wordpress.com/2011/10/05/quiet-hands [accessed 14 February 2021].

Bothe, J. (2020) *'It's torture not therapy: A global overview of conversion therapy: Practices, perpetrators, and the role of states.'* International Rehabilitation Council for Torture Victims. Available at https://irct.org/uploads/media/IRCT_research_on_conversion_therapy.pdf. [accessed 26 April 2021].

Bronstein, S. & Joseph, J. (2011, 10 June) 'Therapy to change "feminine" boy created a troubled man, family says.' CNN. Available at http://edition.cnn.com/2011/US/06/07/sissy.boy.experiment [accessed 14 February 2021].

Brooks, J. (2018) 'The controversial research on "desistance" in transgender youth.' KQED (23 May 2018). Available at www.kqed.org/futureofyou/441784/the-controversial-research-on-desistance-in-transgender-youth [accessed 14 February 2021].

Brown, L.X.Z. (n.d.) 'Living archive & repository on the Judge Rotenberg Center's abuses.' Available at https://autistichoya.net/judge-rotenberg-center [accessed 14 February 2021].

Devita-Raeburn, E. (2016, 11 August) 'Is the most common therapy for autism cruel?' *The Atlantic*. Available at. www.theatlantic.com/health/archive/2016/08/aba-autism-controversy/495272 [accessed 14 February 2021].

de Vries, A.L.C., Noens, I.L.J., Cohen-Kettenis, P.T., van Berckelaer-Onnes, I.A. & Doreleijers, T.A. (2010) 'Autism spectrum disorders in gender dysphoric children and adolescents.' *Journal of Autism Development Disorders*, 40(8), 930–936.

Fox, F. (2015, 8 January) 'Leelah Alcorn's suicide: Conversion therapy is child abuse.' *Time Magazine*. Available at, https://time.com/3655718/leelah-alcorn-suicide-transgender-therapy [accessed 14 February 2021].

Godwin, S. (2015) 'Against parental rights.' *Columbia Human Rights Law Review*, 47(1), 29–36.

Hu, Y., Pereira, A.M., Gao, X., Campos, B.M., Derrington, E. & Corgnet, B. (2021) 'Right temporoparietal junction underlies avoidance of moral transgression in autism spectrum disorder.' *Journal of Neuroscience*, 41(8) 1699–1715.

Jones, R.M., Wheelwright, S., Farrell, K., Martin, E., Green, R. & Di Ceglie, D. (2011) 'Brief report: Female-to-male transsexual people and autistic traits.' *Journal of Autism Development Disorders*, 42(2), 301–306. Available at www.researchgate.net/publication/50908246_Brief_Report_Female-To-Male_Transsexual_People_and_Autistic_Traits/link/02bfe50ca38ca99027000000/download. [accessed 26 April 2021].

Jones, S. (2013). *No You Don't: Essays from an Unstrange Mind* (1st ed.). Unstrange Publications.

Life Magazine (1965) 'Screams, slaps & love: A surprising, shocking treatment helps far-gone mental cripples.' Available at http://neurodiversity.com/library_screams_1965.html [accessed 14 February 2021].

Markram K. & Markram, H. (2010) 'The intense world theory: A unifying theory of the neurobiology of autism.' *Frontiers in Human Neuroscience*, 4, 224.

Rekers, G.A., Bentler, P.M., Rosen, A.C. & Lovaas, O.I. (1977) 'Child gender disturbances: A clinical rationale for intervention.' *Psychotherapy: Theory, Research & Practice*, 14(1), 2–11.

Rekers, G.A. & Lovaas, O.I. (1974) 'Behavioral treatment of deviant sex-role behaviors in a male child.' *Journal of Applied Behavior Analysis*, 7(2), 173–190.

Rekers, G.A., Lovaas, O.I. & Low, B. (1974) 'The behavioral treatment of a "transsexual" preadolescent boy.' *Journal of Abnormal Child Psychology*, 2, 99–116.

Rekers, G.A., Rosen, A. C., Lovaas, O. I. & Bentler, P. M. (1978) 'Sex-role stereotypy and professional intervention for childhood gender disturbance.' *Professional Psychology*, 9, 127–136.

Rowling, J.K. (2020, 10 June) 'J.K. Rowling writes about her reasons for speaking out on sex and gender issues.' Available at www.jkrowling.com/opinions/j-k-rowling-writes-about-her-reasons-for-speaking-out-on-sex-and-gender-issues [accessed 14 February 2021].

Sorbara, J.C., Chiniara, L.N.,Thompson, S. & Palmert, M.R. (2020) 'Mental health and timing of gender-affirming care.' *Pediatrics*, 146(4), e20193600.

Strang, J.F., Powers, M.D., Knauss, M., Sibarium, E., Leibowitz, S.F. & Kenworthy, L. (2018) '"They thought it was an obsession": Trajectories and perspectives of autistic transgender and gender-diverse adolescents.' *Journal of Autism Development ment Disorders*, 48: 4039–4049.

The Lovaas Center, '*Dr. Ivar Lovaas*.' Available at https://thelovaascenter.com/about-us/dr-ivar-lovaas [accessed 14 February 2021], citing Lovaas, O.I. (1987) 'Behavior treatment and normal educational and intellectual functioning in young autistic children.' *Journal of Consulting and Clinical Psychology*, 55(1), 3–9.

The Trevor Project (n.d.) 'About Conversion Therapy.' Available at www.thetrevorproject.org/get-involved/trevor-advocacy/50-bills-50-states/about-conversion-therapy [accessed 14 February 2021].

Troxel v. Granville [2000] 530 US 57, 65.

Warrier, V., Greenberg, D.M., Weir, E., Buckingham, C. *et al.* (2020) 'Elevated rates of autism, other neurodevelopmental and psychiatric diagnoses, and autistic traits in transgender and gender-diverse individuals.' *Nature Communications*, 11(1), 3959.

World Professional Association for Transgender Health (2011) *Standards of Care for the Health of Transsexual, Transgender, and Gender Nonconforming People, 7th Version*, 18–21.

Chapter 4

Autistic Cognition and Gender Identity

REAL STRUGGLES AND IMAGINARY DEFICITS

Reubs J Walsh and David Jackson-Perry

Introduction

Owing to the large overlap between autism and trans and non-binary modalities of gender, there have been numerous attempts by researchers to understand or explain (away) this phenomenon. In this chapter, we critically review a number of such attempts, drawing on the most useful ideas from this literature to provide insights into trans/non-binary autistic lived experience. This provides context and understanding for professionals who encounter autistic trans/non-binary people, enabling them to better account for the specificities of individuals in that overlap, and ultimately better serve the people with whom they work. While the focus of this chapter is the sociocognitive experiences of autistic trans/non-binary people, we would encourage the reader to consider the potential relevance and transferability of this exploration to understanding people of any neurotype, however they identify, as they navigate the choppy seas of gender.

Research into the intersection of autism and gender identity generally considers the large overlap noted earlier as a deviation from a reified norm. The reified norm here is the gender modality[1] (Ashley, 2021) shared by the relatively high proportion of the general population who are cisgender and allistic, the deviation being autistic and/or trans/non-binary people.

In domains so highly contested, complex and controversial as both autism and trans/non-binary identities, research exploring this intersection may inadvertently pursue agendas that are not part of the researchers' intentions. As we explore briefly (and non-exhaustively) below, attempts to describe and explain (away) people who may be both trans/non-binary and autistic tend to appeal to ideas in which trans/non-binary identities are conceptualized as being a secondary effect of autistic symptomatology, and/or loosely mechanistic biological explanations.

Trans/non-binary identities as a secondary effect of autistic symptomatology

Numerous theories purport to explain the elevated rate of trans/non-binary identification among autistic people by reconceptualizing the trans/non-binary identity as a secondary effect of autism. Williams, Allard and Sears (1996, p.641) hypothesized that restricted and repetitive interests may lead autistic males to become preoccupied with a range of things which 'happen to be predominantly feminine in nature'. They give the example of soft fabrics, pointing to sensory differences as a reason for this difference in preference. This theory continues to be discussed in the literature (e.g. van der Meisen *et al.*, 2018). However, leaving aside the debatable question of what is 'feminine in nature', the theory of Williams and co-authors fails to provide any framework for understanding gender identity in general (beyond the assumed invalid identities of autistic trans/non-binary people), or to explain the elevation in rates of trans/non-binary identification in autistic assigned females.

---

1 'Gender modality refers to how a person's gender identity stands in relation to their gender assigned at birth. It is an open-ended category which includes being trans and being cis and welcomes the elaboration of further terms [to trouble the often assumed cis-trans binary]' (Ashley, 2021, p.1).

Other authors (e.g. de Vries *et al.*, 2010; George & Stokes, 2018; Jacobs *et al.*, 2014) lean on the 'rigid thinking' aspects of autism, suggesting that these could lead individuals to misinterpret interests or behaviours that are atypical for their assigned gender as an indication that they are 'in the wrong gender'. This would require us to believe that trans/non-binary autistic people are (mis) identifying as trans/non-binary solely because they are so beholden to stereotypic gender norms that they cannot imagine being a man with feminine interests, for example, and that it is therefore easier to imagine being a woman with a penis, a man with a vulva, or a person whose gender does not conform to either of the majoritarian binary options of man and woman. Clearly, however, these identities each violate the same stereotypic gender norms far more than the alternative. In other words, identifying as trans/non-binary involves rejecting the social narrative about what attributes a given gender identity will be contingent on, and yet it is this same social narrative that is offered as the basis of the rigid thought processes.

Others cite a conceptualization of autism as social impairment to suggest that people who are trans/non-binary come out more readily if they are also autistic: the assumed 'impairment in empathy' of autistic people 'might facilitate them "coming out"...transitioning to their experienced gender, without being prevented by societal prejudices or without being influenced by what other people think about their decision' (Glidden *et al.*, 2016, p.11), a line of thought which is further explored in Chapter 3, where some other approaches are also offered. This is interesting, despite relying on a faulty basis (impairment of empathy is a highly contested area, e.g. Fletcher-Watson & Bird, 2020; Milton, 2012). It implies that there is an unknown number of (presumably allistic) people who do not have this 'impairment' who would come out as being trans/non-binary if they did have it. This clearly renders moot the question of the 'over-representation' of trans/non-binary identities among autistic people given the unknown and unknowable numbers of allistic people who may be trans/non-binary but are 'prevented by societal prejudices' from saying so.

While not directly invalidating the authenticity of the trans/

non-binary identity, this theory strips out the agency of *autistic* trans/non-binary people in seeking authenticity as an intrinsic goal of sufficient value to justify the social costs. It also runs contrary to the existence of an important phenomenon within autism, whereby autistic people perform allistic social behaviour to simplify social interactions for themselves and those with whom they interact. This phenomenon, known as 'camouflaging' and also commonly referred to as masking (which we consider in more detail below), clearly demonstrates that autistic people are both willing and able to alter their behaviour, and even engage in acts of identity concealment, in the pursuit of social harmony.

It has also been suggested that 'Most of the gender-related symptoms in autistic spectrum disorders (ASD) could be related to behavioural and psychological characteristics of autism. For example, a boy with ASD might have a sense of belonging to the female sex after being bullied by male peers', and that this would disrupt identity development (Tateno, Tateno & Saito, 2008, p.238). This is an interesting quote: however inadvertently, 'being bullied by male peers' is positioned here as being an example of the 'behavioural and psychological characteristics of autism'. Presumably, the authors intend this as a reference to the fact that social behaviour perceived by allistic peers as deviant (including, but not limited to, expression of gender diversity) is often used as a pretext for the harassment of autistic youth (Barnett, 2017). It might therefore be more robust to suggest that harassment of peers who do not conform to behavioural expectations is a behavioural and psychological characteristic of allistic youth. Leaving this aside, the authors' hypothesis would predict that autistic people who identify as trans/non-binary do so to escape social ostracism, which contradicts the ample evidence of endemic transphobia in our society (Winter *et al.*, 2016). Further, this theory relegates autistic trans/non-binary gender identities to a product of 'disrupted identity development', while leaving (autistic or allistic) cisgender identities unexplained, unexamined and undisturbed.

These theories rest on the assumption that normative neurotypes ('not being autistic') and cisgender identities are inherently valid and that one of the overlapping non-normativities (being autistic *or* trans) must stem from the other.

Bio-reductive theories

Another version of the same flawed thinking is to assume that there are shared pathophysiological mechanisms giving rise to both autism and trans/non-binary identity. This can be seen in the extreme male brain (EMB) hypothesis of autism aetiology, with its roots in the idea that foetal testosterone is implicated in the neurobiological under-pinnings of autistic neurotypes (c.f. Barbeau, Mendrek & Mottron, 2009; Baron-Cohen, 2002). This further reduces autism (and, subsequently, gender identity) from a complex, highly culturally situated sociocognitive phenomenon to a reductionist, positivist-biological one. The presence of a neurological difference is (mis)taken as an indication that (a) this neurological difference must be the proximal cause of the autism, and (b) that the cause of the neurological difference must belong to the same socially constructed information category, 'biology', rather than, say, an interaction between social and cultural context and cognitive and sensory differences. The primary, 'biological' cause of autism is, according to EMB, the emergence of sexually dimorphic traits of maleness over and above the 'normal' level. Clearly this is predicated on exceptionally flawed and stereotypic conceptions of both typically male and autistic neurobiology and cognition. This line of reasoning has been used to justify the claim that trans/non-binary autistic people who are assigned female at birth are trans/non-binary because of the same foetal testosterone that allegedly caused their autism (Jones *et al.*, 2012): it would be surprising if this same proposed process could explain the same overlap in trans/non-binary and autistic people who were assigned male at birth (Walsh *et al.*, 2018).

Overview of research

We have seen how research largely attempts to explain the gender identities of autistic trans/non-binary people as a symptom or secondary effect of their autism. This inadvertently has various deleterious effects on research and in practice:

1. It unjustifiably prioritizes the assumed reality of a cisgender modality as something that 'just is', as Katz (2007, p.181–182) says of heterosexuality, something not needing explanation or justification. While the phenomenon of gender identity in general might be explicable, it cannot be considered purely in terms of what 'causes' people to be transgender, unless it also considers on an equal footing the factors that 'cause' people to be cisgender.

2. It renders the subjective experience of the person invalid, reading manifestations of trans/non-binary identity (and therefore modality) as being 'symptoms of autism' (Coleman-Smith *et al.*, 2020, p.2). While an identity with a cisgender modality remains unquestioned – it 'just is' – autistic trans/non-binary people are positioned as being 'not really' trans/non-binary (Jackson-Perry, 2020), 'just' autistic.

3. An *a priori* assumption of autistic symptomatology as being a satisfactory explanation for the trans/non-binary modalities of autistic people requires that there be a fundamental qualitative difference between the gender identities of trans/non-binary autistic and allistic people. This difference has not been established.

4. An assumption of autistic deficit closes off all other avenues of enquiry. 'On the ground', in practice, this has serious repercussions. Professionals may be misled into listening to the assumptions that underpin the highly-influential – but in our view misguided – deficit-oriented research, instead of the evidence itself: the person they are trying to support.

Elsewhere in this book (see, for example, Chapters 3, 7 and 8), professionals and service users alike emphasize the importance of listening to – and considering as valid – what the latter are saying. Clearly, the research cited above tends in an opposite direction, so we would now like to consider other theories that we find more useful.

Really trans, really autistic
Imperfect systems, bottom-up processing, and flattened priors

Rather than assume that these marginal identities interact necessarily through mechanisms of deficit, we recognize that the inherent validity of individual experiences are not obviated by deviation from a norm, and that a mechanism that depends on interacting deficits would require (a) that autism be inherently disordered (b) that trans/non-binary identities be inherently disordered and (c) that their co-occurrence invalidates the reality of one or both of those identities. However, a theorization of the high co-occurrence of trans/non-binary modalities with autistic neurotypes that treats trans/non-binary and autistic experiences on their own terms, rather than solely in opposition to the reified norm discussed above, leads to conclusions that validate those experiences.

One earlier example of this approach comes from Kristensen and Broome (2016). They highlight autistic individuals' tendency to use analytical or 'systematizing' approaches to a range of cognitive tasks (Auyeung *et al.*, 2009; Baron-Cohen 2002; Baron-Cohen *et al.*, 2002; Golan & Baron-Cohen, 2006), where allistic individuals would be more likely to employ more intuitive, social context-driven approaches. Systematizing approaches like these describe consistent, rule-bound relationships between concepts or phenomena, representing social interactions as a complex dynamic system, unpredictable due to its complexity, but obeying certain deterministic rules.

Applying this same type of logical reasoning to gender roles as defined by cultural cisgenderism[2] was proposed by Kristensen and Broome (2016) as a route by which autistic people come to perceive cisgenderism as an 'imperfect system' – a system which fails to follow its own rules – which they would consequently reject, and therefore

---

2   'Cisgenderism refers to the ideology that de-legitimizes people's own understanding of their genders and bodies' (Ansara & Berger, 2016, p.231). Cisgenderism is a system of beliefs, values, and assumptions for understanding gender that positions the validity of a gender modality, identity or expression as contingent on conformity to social norms, such as that skirts and dresses are 'feminine' and necessarily worn exclusively by women, that kilts and suits are 'masculine' and that there are only two genders, which are 'opposites'. Cisgenderism therefore leaves no room to comprehend trans and non-binary identities and lives as valid.

be more willing to identify in contradiction to. This approach is based on work which positions systematizing in opposition to empathizing, and which participates in the pathologization of autism, but, pleasingly, declines to import those (false) assumptions along with the (true) realization that autistic people are more prone to use systematizing approaches in general, and with social information (including information about the social construct of gender) in particular.

This is an example of a way in which autistic people may have an advantage when it comes to representing the world around them (and so, perhaps, themselves) in ways that are not considered 'possible' according to categories of sexual and gender norms. Another, similar phenomenon can be observed when considering the way in which people categorize. Categorization is the sorting of objects into groups of entities sharing equivalent properties: people with certain attributes, for example, may be categorized as 'man' or 'woman'. An item is first sensed (a 'low-order' process) and then 'mapped into categories... through bottom-up projections' (categorization being a high-order process, hence 'bottom-up') (Soulières *et al.*, 2007, p.486). The toing-and-froing relationship between these higher- and lower-order processes is mediated by the functional connections between them. Top-down influences (where, for example, pre-existing knowledge, such as category rules, influences the perception of a stimulus at lower levels, e.g. size, shape, etc.) are weaker in autistic people than in allistic people, but *only* in comparison to bottom-up influences (e.g. new information about lower-order perceptual features of a stimulus can influence higher-order perceptual processes, e.g. category rules used when categorizing them into which category they would fall, etc.; Mottron *et al.*, 2006). These (higher-order) categories create expectations (a top-down influence) into which new objects can then be inserted, or not: 'man' and 'woman' may have been learned to be the only forms of gender possible, with a strict set of criteria that must be met by the members of either category. This can be seen as a top-down strategy of perceiving and ordering information that allistic people use.

On the other hand, autistic participants have an 'enhanced ability to disembody targets from surrounding task-irrelevant stimuli'

(Mottron *et al.*, 2006, p.30). In other words, because of the relative strength of their bottom-up projections, while autistic people are *able* to use a top-down strategy of this sort when it is required, they do not *have* to use it unless it is helpful to the task at hand. While we are not aware of any studies directly demonstrating a similar effect regarding social behaviour and perceptions (such as the criteria for 'man' or 'woman'; c.f. Strauss *et al.*, 2011), this is an intriguing proposition. Autistic people, when considering their gender, may be able to do so with less dependence on rigid, pre-existing categories, being instead able to evaluate their own experience relatively accurately even when it lies *outside* the realms of what is generally considered possible.

Bayesian theories of cognition offer similar avenues of exploration (see, e.g., Oaksford & Chater, 2009). Here, the influence of belief (based on past experience) on how you interpret new information is known as the *prior*. Your interpretation of the new information, in light of the prior, is called the *posterior*. The more you tend to assume that your past experience provides valid information about present and future possibilities (i.e. the 'steeper' your prior), the more evidence it will take to convince you of something that contradicts that experience. In other words, a prior is what seems possible based on past experience: in the case of a person assigned male at birth this might be 'People who I have known to have penises are (all or mostly) men: I have a penis: I am therefore a man.' The steeper that prior, the more difficult it will be for contradictory knowledge to become conscious. For this person to recognize themselves as a woman would require a stimulus large enough to overcome that prior.

Pellicano and Burr (2012) proposed that the source of the differences between autistic and allistic people is that autistic people do not have such steep priors; their 'flattened priors' hypothesis suggests past experiences influence present experiences less for autistic than for allistic people. Walsh and colleagues (2018) have applied this to autistic experiences of gender identities, arguing that social conditioning to regard gender as fixed, binary and directly related to genital anatomy (see, e.g., Walsh & Einstein, 2020) is a steep prior for most people living in a society which constructs gender in that way. One is more likely to be able to overcome that prior if it is flattened (reflecting greater uncertainty about what one expects future experiences to be or to mean, and therefore accommodating a broader range of possibilities), which, according to the substantial evidence available, is more the case for autistic than allistic people (e.g. Powell *et al.*, 2016; Skewes & Gebauer, 2016).

In short, autistic people rely less on predictions based on their experiences in the past, and focus more on the moment. This makes them/us more vulnerable to sensory (over/under) stimulation, less willing to make assumptions about the content of other people's minds, and, perhaps, more likely to identify truths which tend to be overlooked by allistic people due to their social conditioning, including truths about themselves: autistic self-insight may function differently, and perhaps in a more precise way.

Autistic self-insight: navigating the choppy seas

Autistic people, as outlined above and in Walsh *et al.* (2018), are thus more likely to be able to notice an incongruity between their gender and that which was assigned to them at birth, and therefore more likely to reject the constraints of cisgender modality. This has the effect of producing in some proportion of autistic people a greater degree of awareness of gender and gendering in social processes (such as interacting with others, or contemplating one's sense of self). This in turn, for many autistic and/or trans/non-binary people, increases the stakes and complexity of the balance between authenticity and pressures to conform – a balance with which allistic people, of all genders, also often struggle.

Tensions between authenticity and safety

As the literature shows, coming out as trans/non-binary and being affirmed in that decision vastly improves mental health outcomes for those who need to do so (e.g. Adams & Liang, 2020; Murad *et al.*, 2010; Olson *et al.*, 2016). Therefore, the ability of autistic cognition to facilitate insight into one's gender identity when it conflicts with the dominant social narrative removes a major barrier to a successful transition. However, autistic people may also, for example, be unable to remain in the closet, even if that is safer – after all, lack of self-knowledge (due not to autism but to social conditioning) is only one among many barriers to a safe and healthy gender transition, and many of the others are also profoundly social, socially complex, and intersect with other challenges autistic people face. Relatedly, it is likely to be very challenging for autistic trans/non-binary people to tolerate some of the compromises that are sometimes made to enable them to be perceived in a *more* gender-congruent fashion, even if it is still inaccurate. These compromises may be especially important for navigating gender as a non-binary person, given the dominant cultural conception of gender as binary (see, e.g., Walsh & Einstein, 2020). As is explored elsewhere in this book (see Chapter 6), it is important for trans/non-binary people to be equipped with the tools to engage in serious self-reflection to truly understand (and embrace) their gender identities, and the limits and possibilities of gender expression in terms of, on the one hand, what is safe and intelligible in a given social space or present society more broadly, and on the other, which aspects of gender expression are essential to well-being. In other words, which compromises are necessary, possible and worthwhile?

A part of this process might be accompanying a person as they consider if, how and to whom they disclose or 'come out'. Disclosure is always a work in progress, and one that, for many people, is never finished but negotiated on an almost daily basis as they meet new people or navigate different spaces. There is no recipe for disclosure, nor is there ever an obligation to disclose. However, early disclosures, and how they are met, are fundamental for a person's short- and long-term well-being, and it is possible to attempt to evaluate disclosures to identify those in which the risk/benefit ratio will be to their advantage. With whom does a service user feel the most comfortable thinking about disclosure? What is it that makes them think that a certain friend, family member, professional or acquaintance would be a good person to disclose to? What are the possible consequences (negative *and* positive) of disclosing to that person? Role play and discussion around these questions might be useful in this context.

Chapter 8 provides further discussion on how to make the relationship with autistic trans and non-binary people a safe, healthy and productive one.

However, while the person that professionals are supporting or working with may need to make compromises, it is important to note that the onus for compromise should not be considered to fall entirely on that person's shoulders. It is vital that professionals work with other individuals in their clients' environments to educate and reassure them, be they peers, parents or professionals. Where possible, all professionals should be ready to leverage their authority to ensure the safety of service users in their social environments, and to support them in asserting their needs.

Tensions, compromises and personal agency

Autistic and/or trans/non-binary people need opportunities – unfortunately rare, even in gender clinics – to discuss and explore identity and attempt to disentangle their own experiences from others' expectations. Therefore, all professionals working with these groups should consider ways in which they can support service users in exploring their subjective experiences of gender and identity. While doing this, clients will need to be supported in countering judgemental thoughts about themselves or from others, to discern for themselves how wider society influences them, and in finding the freedom to accept, reject or find a compromise within that tension. A good compromise is necessarily one that delivers the desired effect in return for what one is giving up. For example, choosing a pronoun because it is easier for others only makes sense if the individual to whom the pronoun refers is comfortable with the pronoun.

Similarly, compromises may not work forever, and service users needn't feel that they arbitrarily have to stick to them if they stop working, become unnecessary or their identity – and therefore their needs – have evolved (see Chapter 7 for more on the importance of being able to reassess decisions on an ongoing basis). For example, a non-binary person might choose to present in a largely femme way to ensure that if they are read as binary, they are read as a woman, as discussed in Chapter 11. However, this might make them more vulnerable to transmisogyny, over and above the transphobia and cis-genderism they're already experiencing. Alternatively, they might find that it works as intended but over time the discomfort of having their gender misread as binary female becomes a new trigger for dysphoria that previously was triggered only by being misread as male. The crucial element is to examine the tensions specific to the individual, their unique identity and their specific context. These are often choppy seas and careful navigation requires mapping out various options. The next step is to identify where the largest moments of gender dysphoria and euphoria occur and prioritize reducing dysphoria and capitalizing on and engaging with euphoria[3] as much as possible, and to try things out. Where safe to do so, professionals should support and encourage the individual to make those in their life aware that these compromises are exploratory and may be subject to change with very little notice.

One such compromise, especially relevant to autistic people, is camouflage. Camouflage describes a social coping mechanism, often involuntary, whereby an autistic person moves towards a more allistic way of communicating. Although their *behaviour* then more closely resembles that of allistic people, the underlying *thought processes* do not. While camouflaging has the advantage of facilitating successful social interactions with allistic people, the heavy demands on executive function and socioemotional cognition can also can also have detrimental effects, especially on mental health and daily functioning (see Mandy, 2019 for an interesting and accessible commentary on this topic). Camouflage is the autistic equivalent of when a trans/non-binary person wears gender-neutral, identity-incongruent clothing that serves mostly to conceal them and their identity. Camouflaging is discussed in more detail in Chapter 10 (where it is referred to as masking). Being autistic and being trans/non-binary can be very

---

3   Gender euphoria refers to 'the positive homologue of gender dysphoria. It speaks to a distinct enjoyment or satisfaction caused by the correspondence between the person's gender identity and gendered features' (Ashley & Ells, 2018, p.24), and 'can be understood in terms of increased subjective well-being associated with gender affirmation' (Bradford, Rider & Spencer, 2019, p.3).

similar experiences in this respect (Adams & Liang, 2020). People who are both autistic and trans/non-binary may be expending considerable amounts of emotional and sociocognitive energy navigating these intersecting and overlapping tensions of authenticity and compromise, existing as they do on the edges of cultural intelligibility.

(Un)intelligibility: culture, coping and consequences

In cultural theory, intelligibility refers to the capacity to properly grasp a concept through reference to, and compatibility with, a shared cultural framework (Butler, 1990). In the context of gender, this means that trans and especially non-binary modalities of gender, which do not fit within the dominant cisgenderist narrative, and perhaps especially when communicated using autistic styles of communication, are not readily understood, because they do not fit within the dominant cultural norms.

It is useful to think about intelligibility in relation to the 'double empathy problem' (Milton, 2012) (the 'double' here refers to each of two people in an interaction), which was also presented in Chapter 2. The dominant, deficit-oriented narrative of autism assumes that the responsibility for misunderstandings involving an autistic and an allistic person lies with 'the autism', or the autistic person. Milton, however, suggests that communication is a two-way street: any communication 'deficit' exists not in the autistic person, but in the *interaction* between two or more people.

The sociocognitive task involved in clear and effective communication is not that the people involved all empathize (and thus communicate) in an allistic way (as a deficit-centred understanding of autism would suggest), but rather that they find a mutually compatible mode of empathizing. In other words, by definition, any time communication between an autistic person and an allistic person goes awry, both parties have failed to empathize effectively with the other. Considering the wider context of autistic people's (mis) treatment in the dominant culture, and the consequent need for behaviours like camouflage, the likelihood is that the autistic person has in many cases already begun to bridge the communication gap.

The allistic person may see their responsibility in that interaction as merely to patiently allow the autistic person to build a bridge, rather than actively to participate in building it.

Therefore, when it comes to navigating gender, and ways of being intelligible without compromising on expressing one's gender in an authentic and fulfilling way, the double empathy problem is doubled again for autistic trans/non-binary people; most of the people in their environment have a different framework for communication, *and* a different framework for understanding gender. Clearly, therefore, autistic people and trans/non-binary people, and especially those who are *both* autistic and trans, face significant hurdles in terms of navigating social interactions, which can cause considerable anxiety. This is a common problem for autistic people, especially for those who are also trans/non-binary and/or LGB (George & Stokes, 2018), and may be an additional barrier to communicating a trans/non-binary identity since trans/non-binary people are often subject to stigma and even shame (Austin & Goodman, 2017; Rood *et al.*, 2016). This may tip the balance in some autistic trans/non-binary people towards compromising on their identity more than is optimal, as social anxiety leads them to prioritize the comfort of others over themselves.

Furthermore, this unavoidable pressure to compromise probably makes people additionally vulnerable to manipulation, both intentional and not. Safeguarding issues are therefore an important consideration when working with this population. For example, trans/non-binary people and autistic women are more likely than their cisgender or neurotypical counterparts (respectively) to have survived sexual assault (Brown-Lavoie, Viecili & Weiss, 2014; James *et al.*, 2016). While it is never the responsibility of a victim to prevent the crime, caring professionals and law enforcement have a duty of care that does extend to helping trans/non-binary autistic people to recognize situations that may pose a disproportionate danger. It is also essential that when crime is reported by autistic trans/non-binary people, their case is handled in a culturally competent manner, their honesty is assumed on the same basis as any other victim of crime, and they are never (even implicitly) blamed for their experience. Furthermore, while social learning detracts less from autistic people's ability to interpret their experiences, social power dynamics remain a powerful source of influence and in any professional–client relationship there is a steep power imbalance, which professionals need to be aware of, and to mitigate wherever possible, especially in interactions with service users.

Advice for practice: three simple rules

- *Be open.* Try to set aside existing discourses that insist on a pathological view of both trans/non-binary and autistic lives, and that deny the reality of an individual's experience, in favour of trusting yourself and your service user to navigate the choppy seas together by casting a critical eye over society's assumptions. With trans/non-binary clients, this also includes such things as not making assumptions about the language they wish to use about their gender identity or body parts. Fundamentally, this means listening to what is being said by the person in front of you.

- *Be clear.* Autistic people can understand communication, but only if it is actually communicated. If it is important that a particular point comes across, make sure to say it directly, literally and kindly. The latter is easy to forget when trying to be direct, and autistic people are just as capable of reading a hint that isn't there as they are of missing a hint that is there – because they've been conditioned to look for hints since missing them has usually caused problems in the past. Similarly (but for different reasons) the experience of being trans/non-binary can lead people to detect hostility that isn't intended, and clarity can help to prevent this. This is also important for trans/non-binary clients because trust in professionals has sadly often been eroded by negative experiences with ignorant or unkind individuals (e.g. Adams *et al.*, 2017). Furthermore, professionals are often working within a system that does not readily facilitate the reality of trans/non-binary lives or the needs of trans/non-binary clients. Therefore, it is crucial to manage expectations, while of course pushing (against the system when necessary) for the best outcome for each client.

- *Be patient.* Being trans/non-binary and being autistic are both exhausting (George & Stokes, 2018). Trans/non-binary people have to struggle against a tide of hatred and incomprehension; autistic people struggle against an ableist social world that painfully and exhaustingly overstimulates them, and blames them for every miscommunication. Both trans/non-binary people and autistic people have elevated rates of health problems, especially stress-related conditions (Cage, Di Monaco & Newell, 2018; Feldman *et al.*, 2016). Therefore, whenever possible, remember that what may appear to be 'unreasonable' behaviour from (a minority of) these clients is often caused by cruelties they experience, with consequences beyond their control, and with its origins in a society that has a long way to go before it will have overcome the cissexism and ablism written into its fabric.

Conclusion

In this chapter, and indeed throughout the book, we have seen the myriad ways in which autistic communication and cognitive styles, and trans/non-binary modalities of gender, are conceptualized as deviations from an arbitrary cultural norm, and in consequence are pathologized and invalidated.[4] We have discussed how autistic trans/non-binary people could best be supported by starting from a critical view of such cultural norms, and how autistic and allistic cognition tends to differ in ways that mean autistic people may also be more inclined to adopt such a critical view, especially when presented with

---

4   It is worth noting here that the identities 'transgender' and 'non-binary' are themselves social constructions framed in the context of white, colonial perceptions of gender that enforce binary gendering from birth, if not earlier. Autistic people from other cultural backgrounds that do not enforce these strict, heteronormative binaries may not have the same experiences of or relationship to them as discussed here (see Chapter 5 in this book for more on this).

evidence that contradicts a cultural norm. In 'coming out', even if only to themselves, *trans/non-binary* autistic people have therefore already begun the critical reconceptualization of a cisgenderist, neurotypical world, and the suggestions for supporting trans people that we have made above are intended to help professionals enable trans/non-binary autistic service users to leverage that 'foot in the door'.

However, while our focus here is on the sociocognitive experiences of autistic trans/non-binary people, the products of the norm-critical approach we take here are of use beyond the specificities. Understanding lives that are outside the 'norm', from a perspective that does not exclusively prioritize or centre normative lives, inevitably leads to better understanding of those normative lives, too. Many of the ideas explored in this chapter will, we hope, therefore enable a deeper understanding of experiences of gender and gendering more broadly.

Autistic and/or trans/non-binary service users need encouragement, support and guidance in negotiating a cisgenderist, neurotypical world. Successful negotiation in this context means minimizing the extent to which they compromise their identity for others' convenience, while also considering safety and intelligibility. This can be done by building on a carefully developed self-awareness of what is coming from the self and what is a non-consensual influence of society. This is especially important for non-binary individuals who may struggle to find ways of being authentic while also existing on the edges of social/cultural intelligibility. However, as Milton (2012) points out, there are at least two people in any interaction, and everybody has shared and equal responsibility to bridge whatever communication gap there is – it is not only autistic people whose empathy is failing when there is a miscommunication between them and an allistic person. Gender expression is of course a form of communication in which autistic trans/non-binary people find themselves with this 'double empathy problem' doubled, by also being trans/non-binary in a cisgenderist culture. Freedom to explore gender expression, to find out what feels the most authentic to oneself, is something that most people in our society could use more of, particularly, perhaps, autistic trans/non-binary people. By being mindful of the social power dynamic of their interactions, professionals who work with autistic trans/non-binary people can create spaces in which this freedom to explore gender is relatively unconstrained.

Equally, though (and we return here to the point made earlier, that the onus for understanding must not lie uniquely with the trans/non-binary autistic person), professionals and clients alike need to recognize that *trans/non-binary people do not owe authenticity of gender* to the cisgenderist world around them. Being authentically trans/non-binary and authentically autistic is not always easy, or safe, so it is important that people can freely choose the right extent for them in a given situation. This is both a life decision (what is the baseline level of authenticity one will express by default), and a skill – of determining in which situations this level of authenticity serves your needs or the needs of others, and when it is appropriate to use coping mechanisms which may involve a different level of authenticity. The core need of this group is, therefore, to be supported in effectively and safely pushing against social power to move towards an authentic way of being both trans/non-binary and autistic.

References

For more of the authors' work, check out their websites at reubs. science and https://pure.qub.ac.uk/en/persons/david-jackson-perry. This is also the easiest way to contact them and to obtain open access to their publications.

Adams, N. & Liang, B. (2020) *Trans and Autistic: Stories from Life at the Intersection.* London: Jessica Kingsley Publishers.

Adams, N., Pearce, R., Veale, J., Radix, A., Castro, D., Sarkar, A., & Thom, K. C. (2017). 'Guidance and ethical considerations for undertaking transgender health research and institutional review boards adjudicating this research.' *Transgender health, 2*(1), 165-175.

Ansara, Y. & Berger, I. (2016) 'Cisgenderism.' In A. Goldberg (ed.), *The SAGE Encyclopedia of LGBTQ Studies.* Thousand Oaks, CA: SAGE Publications.

Ashley, F. (2021) '"Trans" is my gender modality: A modest terminological proposal.' In L. Erickson-Schroth (ed.), *Trans Bodies, Trans Selves* (2nd ed.). Oxford: Oxford University Press.

Ashley, F. & Ells, C. (2018) 'In favor of covering ethically important cosmetic surgeries: Facial feminization surgery for transgender people.' *The American Journal of Bioethics, 18*(12), 23–25. doi:10.1080/15265161.2018.1531162.

Austin, A. & Goodman, R. (2017) 'The impact of social connectedness and internalized transphobic stigma on self-esteem among transgender and gendernon-conforming adults.' *Journal of Homosexuality*, 64(6) 825–841. https://doi.org/10.1080/00 918369.2016.1236587.

Auyeung, B., Wheelwright, S., Allison, C., Atkinson, M., Samarawickrema, N., & Baron-Cohen, S. (2009). 'he Children's Empathy Quotient and Systemizing Quotient: Sex Differences in Typical Development and in Autism Spectrum Conditions.' *Journal of Autism and Developmental Disorders, 39*(11), 1509–1521. https://doi.org/10.1007/s10803-009-0772-x

Barbeau, E.B., Mendrek, A. & Mottron, L. (2009) 'Are autistic traits autistic?' *British Journal of Psychology*, 100(1), 23–28. https://doi.org/10.1348/000712608X337788.

Barnett, J.P. (2017) 'Intersectional harassment and deviant embodiment among autistic adults: (Dis)ability, gender and sexuality.' *Culture, Health & Sexuality*, 19(11), 1210–1224. https://doi.org/10.1080/13691058.2017.1309070.

Baron-Cohen, S. (2002) 'The extreme male brain theory of autism.' *Trends in Cognitive Sciences*, 6(6), 248–254. Retrieved from www.ncbi.nlm.nih.gov/pubmed/12039606.

Baron-Cohen, S., Wheelwright, S., Lawson, J., Griffin, R. & Hill, J. (2002) 'The Exact Mind: Empathising and Systemising in Autism Spectrum Conditions.' In U. Goswami (ed.), *Handbook of Cognitive Development*. Oxford: Blackwell Publishing.

Bradford, N.J., Rider, G.N. & Spencer, K.G. (2019) 'Hair removal and psychological well-being in transfeminine adults: Associations with gender dysphoria and gender euphoria.' *Journal of Dermatological Treatment*, 0(0), 1–8. https://doi.org /10.1080/09546634.2019.1687823.

Brown-Lavoie, S.M., Viecili, M.A. & Weiss, J. A. (2014) 'Sexual knowledge and victimization in adults with autism spectrum disorders.' *Journal of Autism and Developmental Disorders*, 44(9), 2185–2196.

Butler, J. (1990) *Gender Trouble: Feminism and the Subversion of Identity*. London: Routledge.

Cage, E., Di Monaco, J. & Newell, V. (2018) 'Experiences of autism acceptance and mental health in autistic adults.' *Journal of Autism and Developmental Disorders*, 48(2), 473–484. https://doi.org/10.1007/s10803-017-3342-7.

Coleman-Smith, R.S., Smith, R., Milne, E. & Thompson, A.R. (2020) '"Conflict versus Congruence": A qualitative study exploring the experience of gender dysphoria for adults with autism spectrum disorder.' *Journal of Autism and Developmental Disorders*, 50: 2643–2657. https://doi.org/10.1007/s10803-019-04296-3.

de Vries, A.L.C., Noens, I.L.J., Cohen-Kettenis, P.T., van Berckelaer-Onnes, I.A. & Doreleijers, T.A. (2010) 'Autism spectrum disorders in gender dysphoric children and adolescents.' *Journal of Autism and Developmental Disorders*, 40(8), 930–936. https://doi.org/10.1007/s10803-010-0935-9.

Feldman, J., Brown, G.R., Deutsch, M.B., Hembree, W. *et al.* (2016) 'Priorities for transgender medical and healthcare research.' *Current Opinion in Endocrinology, Diabetes, and Obesity*, 23(2), 180–187. https://doi.org/10.1097/ MED.0000000000000231.

Fletcher-Watson, S. & Bird, G. (2020) 'Autism and empathy: What are the real links?' *Autism*, 24(1), 3–6. https://doi.org/10.1177/1362361319883506.

George, R. & Stokes, M. A. (2018). 'Gender identity and sexual orientation in autism spectrum disorder.' *Autism*, 22(8), 970–982. https://doi.org/10.1177/1362361317714587.

Glidden, D., Bouman, W.P., Jones, B.A. & Arcelus, J. (2016) 'Gender dysphoria and autism spectrum disorder: A systematic review of the literature.' *Sexual Medicine Reviews*, 4(1), 3–14. https://doi.org/10.1016/j.sxmr.2015.10.003.

Golan, O., & Baron-Cohen, S. (2006). 'Systemizing empathy: Teaching adults with Asperger syndrome or high-functioning autism to recognize complex emotions using interactive multimedia.' *Development and Psychopathology, 18(02)*, 591–617. https://doi.org/10.1017/S0954579406060305

Jackson-Perry, D. (2020) 'The autistic art of failure? Unknowing imperfect systems of sexuality and gender.' *Scandinavian Journal of Disability Research*, 22(1), 221–229. http://doi.org/10.16993/sjdr.634.

Jacobs, L.A., Rachlin, K., Erickson-Schroth, L. & Janssen, A. (2014) 'Gender dysphoria and co-occurring autism spectrum disorders: Review, case examples, and treatment considerations.' *LGBT Health*, 1(4), 277–282.

James, S.E., Herman, J.L., Rankin, S., Keisling, M., Mottet, L. & Anafi, M. (2016) *The Report of the 2015 U.S. Transgender Survey*. Washington, DC: National Center for Transgender Equality.

Jones, R.M., Wheelwright, S., Farrell, K., Martin, E. *et al.* (2012) 'Brief report: Female-to-male transsexual people and autistic traits.' *Journal of Autism Development Disorder*, 42, 301–306. https://doi.org/10.1007/s10803-011-1227-8.

Katz, J.N. (2007) *The Invention of Heterosexuality*. Chicago, IL: University of Chicago Press.

Kristensen, Z. E., & Broome, M. R. (2016). 'Autistic Traits in an Internet Sample of Gender Variant UK Adults.' *International Journal of Transgenderism, 2739(July)*, 234–245. https://doi.org/10.1080/15532739.2015.1094436.

Mandy W. (2019) 'Social camouflaging in autism: Is it time to lose the mask?' *Autism*, 23(8), 1879–1881. doi:10.1177/1362361319878559.

Milton, D.E.M. (2012) 'On the ontological status of autism: The "double empathy problem".' *Disability & Society*, 27(6), 883–887. https://doi.org/10.1080/0968759 9.2012.710008.

Mottron, L., Dawson, M., Soulières, I., Hubert, B. & Burack, J. (2006) 'Enhanced perceptual functioning in autism: An update, and eight principles of autistic perception.' *Journal of Autism and Developmental Disorders*, 36(1), 27–43.

Murad, M.H., Elamin, M.B., Garcia, M.Z., Mullan, R.J. *et al.* (2010) 'Hormonal therapy and sex reassignment: A systematic review and meta-analysis of quality of life and psychosocial outcomes.' *Clinical Endocrinology*, 72(2), 214–231. https://doi.org/10.1111/j.1365-2265.2009.03625.x.

Oaksford, M. & Chater, N. (2009) 'Précis of Bayesian rationality: The probabilistic approach to human reasoning.' *Behavioral and Brain Sciences*, 32(01), 69–84. https://doi.org/10.1017/S0140525X09000284

Olson K. R., Durwood L., & DeMeules M., & McLaughlin, K. A. (2016). 'Mental health of transgender children who are supported in their identities.' *Pediatrics, 137(3)*, e20153223.

Pellicano, E. & Burr, D. (2012) 'When the world becomes "too real": A Bayesian explanation of autistic perception.' *Trends in Cognitive Sciences*, 16(10), 504–510.

Powell, G., Meredith, Z., McMillin, R. & Freeman, T.C.A. (2016) 'Bayesian models of individual differences: Combining autistic traits and sensory thresholds to predict motion perception.' *Psychological Science*, 27(12), 1562–1572. https://doi.org/10.1177/0956797616665351.

Rood, B.A., Reisner, S.L., Surace, F.I., Puckett, J.A., Maroney, M.R. & Pantalone, D.W. (2016) 'Expecting rejection: Understanding the minority stress experiences of transgender and gender-nonconforming individuals.' *Transgender Health*, 1(1), 151–164. https://doi.org/10.1089/trgh.2016.0012.

Skewes, J.C. & Gebauer, L. (2016) 'Brief report: Suboptimal auditory localization in autism spectrum disorder: Support for the Bayesian account of sensory symptoms.' *Journal of Autism and Developmental Disorders*, 46(7), 2539–2547. https://doi.org/10.1007/s10803-016-2774-9.

Soulières, I., Mottron, L., Saumier, D. & Larochelle, S. (2007) 'Atypical categorical perception in autism: Autonomy of discrimination.' *Journal of Autism and Developmental Disorders*, 37(3), 481–490. https://doi.org/10.1007/s10803-006-0172-4.

Strauss, M. S., Newell, L. C., Best, C. A., Hannigen, S. F., Gastgeb, H. Z., & Giovannelli, J. L. (2012). 'The development of facial gender categorization in individuals with and without autism: The impact of typicality.' *Journal of Autism and Developmental Disorders*, 42(9), 1847–1855. https://doi.org/10.1007/s10803-011-1428-1

Tateno, M., Tateno, Y. & Saito, T. (2008) 'Comorbid childhood gender identity disorder in a boy with Asperger syndrome.' *Psychiatry and Clinical Neurosciences*, 62(2), 238–238.

van der Miesen, A.I.R., de Vries, A.L.C., Steensma, T.D. & Hartman, C.A. (2018) 'Autistic symptoms in children and adolescents with gender dysphoria.' *Journal of Autism and Developmental Disorders*, 48(5), 1537–1548. https://doi.org/10.1007/s10803-017-3417-5.

Walsh, R. & Einstein, G. (2020) *Transgender Embodiment: A Feminist, Situated Neuroscienceperspective*. Preprint available: https://doi.org/10.13140/RG.2.2.28512.64008.

Walsh, R.J., Krabbendam, L., Dewinter, J. & Begeer, S. (2018) 'Brief report: Gender identity differences in autistic adults: Associations with perceptual and socio-cognitive profiles.' *Journal of Autism and Developmental Disorders*, 48(12), 4070–4078. https://doi.org/10.1007/s10803-018-3702-y.

Williams, P.G., Allard, A.M. & Sears, L. (1996) 'Case study: Cross-gender preoccupations in two male children with autism.' *Journal of Autism and Developmental Disorders*, 26(6), 635–642.

Winter, S., Diamond, M., Green, J., Karasic, D., Reed, T., Whittle, S. & Wylie, K. (2016) 'Transgender people: Health at the margins of society.' *The Lancet*, 388(10042), 390–400.

Chapter 5

Trans, Autistic and BIPOC

LIVING AT THE INTERSECTIONS OF AUTISM, RACE AND GENDER DIVERSITY

Taylor René Kielsgard and Lydia X.Z. Brown

Introduction

What does it mean to be autistic, trans and negatively racialized? As autistic advocates who have lived at the intersections, our stories are complex, fraught and, at times, difficult to tell. As Jim Sinclair an autism rights movement activist and co-founder of the Autism Network International (ANI), cautioned long ago, it's often too easy for us to feel trapped in the exploitative 'self-narrating zoo exhibit' framing, where non-disabled people demand the most invasive and intimate details from our personal life stories, but refuse to invite or consider our political analysis, demands and organizing (Raymaker, 2019). At the same time, telling our stories can be a powerful act of taking control of our narratives and leaving evidence 'that we were here, that we existed, that we survived and loved and ached'.[1]

Both of us are multiply neurodivergent and disabled autistic advocates who have complicated relationships with gender and race in our own lives. We offer brief glimpses into our stories here, in hopes that they might stir you and spur you to realization, recognition or action. Beyond those glimpses, we offer reflections on the current

---

[1]   This quote appears on the sidebar of queer, Korean, disabled organizer Mia Mingus's website *Leaving Evidence*, at https://leavingevidence.wordpress.com/about-2.

state of community advocacy and research affecting autistic trans people of colour, and suggestions for what professionals, researchers and policy makers can do to better support our community members.

A glimpse of Taylor's story

I was in my fifties before I felt comfortable coming out as non-binary. I had known since childhood that I didn't always fit into the stereo-typical definition of what being a girl supposedly means, and I had dealt with so much trauma from being punished for trying to reject conventional femininity. At one point, my mother was disappointed and got upset because I rejected a Christmas gift of a baby doll. She told me that I couldn't be both a 'tomboy and a girly girl'. I kept trying to explain that I didn't always feel completely one way or the other and that I felt more like a person and not just a girl or tomboy, but I didn't know how to explain exactly how I felt so these conversations with my mother were not productive.

Gender became even more confusing when I became a parent, because being a mother is extremely gendered as a feminine or women's experience. I've been talking for years to a close friend about this, sometimes spending hours and hours on the phone at a time. Both of us have known we're non-binary for years, but we didn't know how to describe it when we've also considered ourselves mothers and when that has been so important to us. With parenting, everything seems tied to gender – you're either a mum or a dad, but not just a parent.

I began experiencing extreme body dysphoria when I decided to breastfeed after my children were born. I had always been small-breasted, which never was an issue for me. I actually felt comfortable being tiny, but when my breasts became large after my milk came in, I experienced extreme body dysphoria and had intermittent bouts of situational depression. I didn't feel as if I fitted inside my body anymore. Although I continued breastfeeding, it was an overwhelming experience for me and caused me to question even more the disconnect I had always experienced as it relates to physical appearance and gender stereotypes.

Gender still feels so complicated in my brain that I don't know how to explain it fully, and I still feel as if I'm putting pieces together. Even today, I still use both she/her and they/them pronouns because I find myself internally confused about binary stereotypes when it comes to parenthood as someone with a uterus. I was born in a generation that not only didn't recognize gender as anything other than male or female, but that punished you if you even dared to try claiming a different notion of gender.

My relationship with my racial identity is also complicated, as an unenrolled mixed-race Native and white person – I know who my ancestors were and grew up near my people, but my grandparents chose not to include us on the tribal rolls out of legitimate concern for our safety. Due to the many conflicts, trauma and issues about relationships, appropriation and passing privilege that can surround multi-racial identities, however, I'm not always comfortable opening up in detail about this part of my life outside close relationships. It's important to me to support more visible autistic people of colour to be in leadership and public advocacy positions.

A glimpse of Lydia's story

I too knew from a young age that I wasn't a girl or a boy, but didn't have words to explain it until I was out of high school and in college. When I was a kid, I remember getting equally excited about the idea of wearing both feminine-coded clothing like ball gowns and peasant skirts and masculine-coded clothing like tuxedos, ties and cravats. I loved the idea of wearing long, styled hair, and also growing a long, combed beard. I played imagination games and wrote fiction from the perspectives of women and men characters – but never felt at home with expectations for either femininity or masculinity.

Today, when thinking about gender, it's more accurate to say that I'm agender or genderless than anything else – gendervague (e.g. Brown, 2019; Neumeier, 2015) (meaning being autistic and otherwise neurodivergent shapes my relationship to gender), genderqueer (meaning my gender feels queer, disruptive and subversive) and non-binary (meaning my gender is something other than woman or man) are all technically correct, but don't fully capture who I am or how I relate to gender. (Which is to say, I don't.) As so many other autistic people often say, sometimes even in the same words, I don't feel like a gender; I feel like me (Kourti & MacLeod, 2019).

My relationship to race and culture is also complex. I am one of thousands of people of colour who were transracially and transnationally adopted from predominantly black, brown and Asian nations into mostly white families in the United States and other western or Global North nations. I am East Asian, and specifically Chinese. I lack connection and grounding in either Chinese communities in China or in diasporic Chinese American communities. Though they tried their best to instil appreciation for my ancestral heritage and culture, it's impossible to replicate an upbringing in one cultural environment in a different one. Many adult transracial/transnational adoptees of colour similarly describe lack, loss, denial and deprivation. In my adult life, I am most politically at home among sick, mad, neurodivergent and disabled queer and trans people of colour – keenly aware of both the impact of marginalization and oppression in my life, as well as forms of privilege and access to resources I have had as a light-skinned citizen fluent in spoken English.

What's on my mind most these days is the horrific legacies of intergenerational and collective trauma visited on those of us who live at the margins of the margins – no matter what tenuous hold we may have to some resources or (at least conditionally) privileged experiences, just sitting with the knowledge and understanding that even this conversation is incredibly limited. It's impossible to sever my racial, gender or disabled identities or experiences from one another – to talk about them in isolation, out of context. We are all complex multifaceted human beings. And as Audre Lorde (who was brilliantly black, queer and disabled) taught us, 'There is no such thing as a single-issue struggle because we do not live single-issue lives' (Lorde, 2007, p.138).

Intersection of trans and autistic identities

While we do know that autistic people are more likely to identify as trans than non-autistic people, and that trans people are more likely to be autistic than cisgender people, there isn't a lot of research yet on the intersection of autistic and trans identities and experiences. What little research we have tends to be clinically oriented, with fewer qualitative studies or ethnographic research. Such clinical research tends to consist of psychologists and other medical professionals providing data from a medicalized perspective, and does not typically include autistic trans people as collaborators or co-investigators, or even as paid participants. Some research is clinically focused but increasingly involving autistic and trans collaborators as co-investigators and co-authors (Strang *et al.*, 2018; Strang *et al.*, 2020). Emerging research is beginning to change that reality, but has only started to do so within recent years, along with the publication of several new books by openly trans autistic people about living at the intersections of neurodivergence and transness, though fewer autistic trans people of colour are publishing than white autistic trans people (e.g. Adams & Liang, 2020; Dale, 2019; Gratton, 2019; Sparrow, 2020).[2]

Cisgender and non-autistic people have posed many of their own, largely pathologizing, theories as to why autistic people are more likely to be trans, gender non-conforming, or non-binary. In particular, the 'extreme male brain' theory of autism claims that autistic people tend to be 'systemizers' rather than 'empathizers', and that systemizing is an inherently hypermasculine trait (Yergeau, 2020). This theory not only upholds harmful and essentialist ideas about gender, but also erases the existence of autistic transfeminine people and particularly autistic trans women. These theories, and their implications, were discussed in more detail in Chapters 3 and 4. Many of us, however, have a quite different sense of why so many autistic people are trans and willing to come out as such. For many of us, it may be that we are already accustomed to being seen as the other and, therefore, it can feel easier in some ways to realize and accept that we may not conform to gender norms and the expectation to be cisgender either. For others, it can be that being autistic means that we do not understand gender in the same way as neurotypical people – even if

---

2   Writing by several autistic trans people of colour also appears in Brown, Ashkenazy & Onaiwu (2017), in *Monstering Magazine*, and in the *Barking Sycamores* and *Spoon Knife Anthology* collections under N.I. Nicholson's editorship.

we intellectually understand the concepts of binary genders, they may not match our internal understanding of ourselves, as discussed in various chapters throughout this book. In some parts of the autistic community, it's actually harder to find straight cisgender people than it is to find queer and trans people. In fact, the main reason that the US-based non-profit Autistic Women & Nonbinary Network (AWN)[3] decided to change its name in 2018 from the original name Autism Women's Network is because the board wanted to better represent its large number of non-binary and trans leaders and community members.[4]

Intersections of trans and negatively racialized identities

Trans people of colour – particularly black, brown, and Native trans women – are at extraordinarily high risk for violence, criminalization and abuse (e.g. Martinez & Law, 2019). As late as February 2021, New York State finally repealed its decades-old law banning loitering with the intent to engage in sex work, that had long been used to profile and detain trans women (particularly trans women of colour) as presumptively criminal whether or not they were sex workers – leading to escalated sexual abuse in jails and prisons (Yurcaba, 2021). In several states, people accused of violent crimes up to and including murder can raise a 'trans panic defence', claiming that a victim's

---

3   Both of the authors of this chapter are involved with AWN. Founded in 2010, AWN focuses on both neurodiversity as well as gender justice and trans liberation. AWN is a partner or consultant on multiple research projects through academic-community partnerships, including research projects and other engagements with the Children's National Hospital, Brooklyn Law School, Rice University, Duke University, George Washington University, University of Michigan, Georgia State University, Bellevue College, the University of Houston and the University of Texas.

4   Not all non-binary people consider themselves to be trans, though many do. We use an expansive definition of trans throughout this chapter to include both people who affirmatively identify as trans, and any people who do not identify with the gender and sex they were assigned at birth.

gender identity causes and therefore justifies violence toward them.[5] Experiences of violence are further compounded by systematic and disproportionate lack and deprivation of resources, visibility and representation for trans people of colour as compared to white trans people (Harrison-Quintana, Lettman-Hicks & Grant, 2011).

Further complicating analysis of intersecting racism and anti-trans oppression, many communities of colour have particular terminology and concepts in our cultures for gender experiences that are not conceptualizable within the white-centric notion of the gender binary. For instance, in a culture where there have always been three genders, the idea that a person of the third gender is transgender no longer makes sense, since the term transgender was created to mean a person whose understanding of their own gender does not match the gender and sex assigned at birth. In other words, to be understood as transgender requires a person to have been assumed to be or assigned as a gender and sex at birth that does not match the gender with which that person identifies later. People whose understanding of their gender – and whose community's understanding of their gender – has always been of a gender that is not girl or boy, may not consider themselves to be transgender in the same way as people whose understanding of their gender directly contradicts the assumptions made about their gender by others.

Globally, white, western, colonizing notions of gender as a binary have uprooted and devastated whole communities of negatively racialized people, many of whose cultures have always already recognized and honoured gender experiences outside the binary. Whether for hijras in India, kathoey and phuying praphet song in Thailand, baklâ, bayot, or agî people in the Philippines, māhū in Hawaii, okule and agule people in the Lugbara community, or muxes in Juchitán, the concepts of third genders, mixed genders and gender fluidity have long existed in many societies and cultures in the Global South (e.g. Collins, 2017; binaohan, 2014; Jackson & Shanks, 2017; Tikuna &

---

5 For an updated list of states with passed or proposed legislation banning 'gay panic' and 'trans panic' defences, see *LGBTQ+ Panic Defense*, The National LGBT Bar Association. Available at https://lgbtbar.org/programs/advocacy/gay-trans-panic-defense [accessed 26 April 2021].

Lavinas Picq, 2019). Many Native/Indigenous people within what is currently the US and Canada, for instance, use the term 'two spirit' to refer to Native/Indigenous people whose genders or sexualities do not conform to white, colonizing strictures and expectations. Some Native/Indigenous people use two spirit to reference queer sexuality (e.g. non-heterosexuality), while others use it to reference an understanding of gender identities and roles beyond the colonizing, white-centric notion of the gender binary (Raphaelito *et al.*, 2019).

Intersections of trans, autistic, and negatively racialized communities

Most representation of autism is of white autistic people, which already diminishes the existence and needs of autistic people of colour – even though we are a global majority within the autistic community. Likewise, the trans community has long centred specific types of trans people – namely, non-disabled, white, thin, conventionally attractive and ambiguously androgynous or transmasculine people. Disabled trans people and trans people of colour remain at the margins even within trans spaces. Making matters worse, the dominant narrative of autism is that all autistic people are either de-gendered and infantilized, or presumed cisgender by default. Arguments by anti-trans campaigners that autistic youth are being brainwashed or manipulated into adopting trans identities further rely on the ableist presumption of incompetence, which can have real and devastating consequences in our lives.

An acquaintance of one of the authors was pressured to leave a trans youth support group because its members and support staff did not know how to include a person with intellectual disabilities. Several of our colleagues and friends have faced persistent misgendering and deadnaming in psychiatric hospitals, and conflation of gender dysphoria with their psychiatric disabilities. We have heard chilling stories from some of our colleagues and friends about pressure from professionals to seek cure-oriented treatment from autism as a precondition for accessing gender-affirming care, including gender-confirmation surgeries.

For our community members to have any real chance of accessing care, receiving support and living authentically and freely – let alone accessing healing – we need change urgently. The entire social services, education and healthcare systems must change to focus on human need as determined by those who are most impacted and therefore have the most to lose. Ending systemic, structural and institutional oppression will not happen overnight, but we can begin to move in the right direction by listening to what autistic trans people of colour have been saying all along both about what is wrong now and about what can change for the better.

Considerations and recommendations for professionals

We know that we are in the long haul as we labour for truly transformative change and liberation. We also recognize that our community members are in crisis now, and we cannot wait until the perfect world materializes to start practising justice. With this in mind, we offer the following starting points for professionals and other community members to consider when working with or supporting autistic trans people of colour.

Presume competence

Far too often, autistic trans people of colour struggle to access gender-affirming support and treatment, including elements of both social and medical transition. Our experiences of gender dysphoria (for those of us who experience it) are often dismissed by the very professionals whose support we need in order to access various forms of transition – legal name and gender marker changes, recognition of chosen names and pronouns, hormonal treatment, puberty blockers for youth, and gender-confirmation surgery, among others. Autistic people are not automatically incompetent, even when we are young, or when we have intellectual disabilities and psychosocial disabilities, or when we communicate by typing instead of talking, as was further discussed in Chapter 3. Presume that we are competent to understand our own lives, bodies, experiences and identities.

Understand that we live this every day – we know what we are talking about, because we are inside our bodies and minds 100 per cent of the time. As a non-binary parent, Taylor knows how scary and distresssing it can be to experience natural hormonal and physical changes just from breastfeeding their children. Another acquaintance experiencing gender dysphoria shared with Taylor that they contemplated suicide when their child was only six months old because they worried they'd be judged for quitting breastfeeding even though the experience was extremely dysphoric. If a person is experiencing dysphoria, they need to know that they will be believed and supported in taking the steps necessary to minimize it.

Humanize trans experiences

People of colour, trans people and autistic (and other disabled) people have shared histories and experiences of intense pathologization, up to and including medical incarceration and experimentation. It's no wonder that trans communities have fought long and hard to stop the use of pathologizing and dehumanizing terminology, including fighting for removal of trans identities and experiences from classification manuals of mental illnesses and diseases. (Unfortunately, such activism has often been steeped in ableism, as non-disabled trans people often state that trans people should be respected based on not being mentally ill – an assertion that justifies pathologization of disabled people.)

Yet for specific legal and medical purposes, it can be okay to use otherwise pathologizing labels (like gender dysphoria or gender identity disorder) or language, with an individual trans person's consent to do so. For instance, for some trans people in prison (who are disproportionately disabled and people of colour), using pathologizing language on paperwork is a necessary prerequisite for successfully obtaining a legal name change or gender marker change, or access to gender-specific clothing while incarcerated. At the same time, it's particularly important not to criminalize mental health and psychosocial disabilities – trans people of colour are already more likely to experience dangerous or deadly police force, and to experience arrest and incarceration.

Enable non-gendered support groups

Assuming that all autistic youth and adults can only participate in support groups if they are gendered as women's/girl's or men's/boy's support groups serves to exclude not only non-binary autistic people, but autistic trans women and men who are not necessarily comfortable disclosing or outing their gender identity, as well as autistic people of colour whose genders do not map onto a binary split. A better solution is to offer non-gendered support groups, with the option for people to self-identify on their own to form separate groups based on affinity with a specific gender identity or experience, or a set of gender identities, if they wish to do so. Such gender-specific groups should never be mandated with social services or therapy programmes.

Defend trans youth, clients and co-workers

If you are in a position of at least some power or influence – whether as a professional, educator, supervisor or service provider – it is your responsibility to defend and support trans people experiencing bullying, abuse or ostracism. If trans people whom you work with have publicly asked for others to use a chosen name and/or different pronouns from the ones other people have used for them before, insist that teachers, administrators and other professionals use their correct names and pronouns. If you are not sure whether a particular trans person would like you to do this, you can and should ask whether you should use a different name and pronoun set when talking about them to their parents or other family members, versus other people in your clinical practice or school, or in other settings. This is particularly helpful for autistic trans people, since we tend to operate better with clear, explicit parameters. It may also be a matter of safety not to have a chosen name or pronouns used in conversations with family members. These issues are also further discussed in Chapter 8.

Support trans people in accessing gendered spaces that match their gender

Too often, trans people are singled out as a separate category from women and men, or girls and boys. Even dropdown forms and routine paperwork often offer the options 'female', 'male' and 'transgender', which both erases non-binary people and forces trans women and trans men to decide between affirming their gender or disclosing their status as trans. Trans women, trans men and non-binary trans people sometimes do want to participate in gender-specific activities or visit gender-specific spaces, and we should have access to the spaces that match our genders. Autistic trans people who want to participate in sports, for instance, should be able to participate in sports teams and leagues that match their gender.

Help advocate for trans people when they are at risk of losing their jobs

Autistic trans people of colour face the compounded effects of disability, gender and race on likelihood of temporary or chronic unemployment, under-employment and precarious employment. The very real possibility of overt discrimination and hostile work environments makes it even more likely that we will face job loss at various points throughout our lives. If you are a professional working with autistic trans people of colour, know that we need support and advocacy with employers when our jobs are at risk. Defer to a particular person about what tactics and strategies might be most productive and helpful in a specific situation. At the same time, know that because of racism, ableism and anti-trans oppression, professionals who do not share our identities are much more likely to be taken seriously than we are – and we are painfully aware of this reality.

Provide support for executive functioning, and recognize structural inequities

When autistic trans people of colour need assistance with time and cognitive labour-intensive tasks like applying for housing subsidies, filing employment discrimination complaints, renewing public benefits eligibility, applying for federal student financial aid, changing health insurance plans and obtaining new identification documents, we likely will need significant support around executive dysfunction common for many autistic people. Different strategies will work differently for different people, but nearly all of us need some external accountability, prompting and support to be able to complete these tasks. For autistic trans people of colour experiencing housing instability, working multiple jobs at a time or surviving natural disasters, ability to follow through on paperwork-heavy tasks and processes can deteriorate even further. Be prepared for missed deadlines, late responses to phone calls or emails, forgotten or abandoned tasks, lost paperwork and forgotten information – these are frequent and natural consequences of executive dysfunction, depression and chronic sustained burnout conditions common in multiply marginalized disabled people's lives.

Remember that autistic trans people of colour are partners and collaborators

We are not simply research subjects, or people affected by laws and policies, or clients who receive services. Effective, culturally responsive policy making and research requires collaboration and partnership with autistic trans people of colour both as individuals and as representatives and leaders of organizations and coalitions from our communities. Researchers should consider adopting community-based participatory action research models which prioritize shaping and designing research objectives that align with goals and interests of directly impacted communities.

Decriminalize survival and existence

Fight to decriminalize our existence and survival. Repealing 'trans panic defence' laws and laws that criminalize HIV status, sex work, homelessness and drug use will all go a long way towards decarceration and de-institutionalization. Fighting to get all our people free, fed, housed and clothed also means challenging and ending the expansion and existence of spaces like disability-specific institutions as well as penal institutions where autistic trans people of colour are much more likely to be incarcerated and subjected to repeated violence. Liberation is not a metaphor.

Understand the significance and pervasiveness of trauma

Because we face disproportionate rates of homelessness, criminalization, sexual and domestic violence, unemployment and other forms of interpersonal and structural violence, we are nearly all survivors of multiple and compounded traumas. As autistic people, we will inevitably be on both ends of communication mistakes as well as more serious conflict, which require understanding and compassion from those around us – including support in taking accountability when necessary, with attention to and care for trauma in the process. Remember that we fight for liberation because we wish one day to live in a world where we no longer have to fear violence, deprivation or devastation. Our daily lives are marked by historical, intergenerational, collective and compounded individual traumas that affect our relationships and interactions with others and with ourselves.

References

Adams, N. & Liang, B. (2020) *Trans and Autistic: Stories from Life at the Intersection.* London: Jessica Kingsley Publishers.

binaohan, b. (2014) *Decolonizing Trans/gender* 101. Biyuti Press.

Brown, L.X.Z. (2019, 22 June) *Gendervague: At the intersection of autistic and trans experiences.* National LGBTQ Task Force. Available at https://web.archive.org/web/20190411000916/https://thetaskforceblog.org/2016/06/22/gendervague-at-the-intersection-of-autistic-and-trans-experiences [accessed 27 April 2021].

Brown, L.X.Z., Ashkenazy, E. & Onaiwu, M.G. (eds) (2017) *All the Weight of Our Dreams: On Living Racialized Autism.* Lincoln, NE: DragonBee Press.

Collins, S. (2017, 17 October) *The splendor of gender non-conformity in Africa.* Available at https://medium.com/@janelane_62637/the-splendor-of-gender-non-conformity-in-africa-f894ff5706e1 [accessed 27 April 2021].

Dale, L.K. (2019) *Uncomfortable Labels: My Life as a Gay Autistic Trans Woman.* London: Jessica Kingsley Publishers.

Gratton, F.V. (2019) *Supporting Transgender Autistic Youth and Adults: A Guide for Professionals and Families* London: Jessica Kingsley Publishers.

Harrison-Quintana, J., Lettman-Hicks, S. & Grant, J. (2011, September) *Injustice at Every Turn: A look at Black Respondents in the National Transgender Discrimination Survey.* National Black Justice Coalition, National Center for Transgender Equality, & National LGBTQ Task Force. Available at www.transequality.org/sites/default/files/docs/resources/ntds_black_respondents_2.pdf [accessed 27 April 2021].

Jackson, k. & Shanks, M. (2017) *Decolonizing Gender: A Curriculum.* Available at www.decolonizinggender.com/the-zine [accessed 27 April 2021].

Kourti, M. & MacLeod, A. (2019) '"I don't feel like a gender, I feel like myself": Autistic individuals raised as girls exploring gender identity.' *Autism in Adulthood*, 1.1.

LGBTQ+ Panic Defense, The National LGBT Bar Association. Available at https://lgbtbar.org/programs/advocacy/gay-trans-panic-defense [accessed 27 April 2021].

Lorde, A. (2007) 'Learning from the 60s.' In *Sister Outsider: Essays and Speeches.* Berkeley, CA: Crossing Press.

Martinez, G. & Law, T. (2019, 12 June) 'Two recent murders of black trans women in Texas reveal a nationwide crisis, advocates say.' *Time Magazine.* Available at https://time.com/5601227/two-black-trans-women-murders-in-dallas-anti-trans-violence [accessed 27 April 2021].

Neumeier, S.M. (2015, 19 June) *Disabled Genders. Silence Breaking Sound.* Available at https://silencebreakingsound.wordpress.com/2015/06/19/disabled-genders/comment-page-1/#comment-168 [accessed 27 April 2021].

Raphaelito, J. (Diné, Navajo Nation), Peter, K. (Diné, Navajo Nation), Red Shirt, M. (Oglala Lakota) & Young, R. (Lac du Flambeau Ojibwe) (2019) *Indigenizing Love: A Toolkit for Native Youth to Build Inclusion.* Western States Center, Tribal Sovereignty Program. Available at www.healthynativeyouth.org/wp-content/uploads/2019/09/IndigenizingLoveToolkitYouth.pdf [accessed 27 April 2021].

Raymaker, D. (2009, 22 January) *Self-narrating zoo exhibits, walking autism textbooks, and other beasts to beware.* Available at http://doraraymaker.com/change/2009/01/22/self-narrating-zoo-exhibits-walking-autism-textbooks-and-other-beasts-to-beware.

Sparrow, M. (ed.) (2020) *Spectrums: Autistic Transgender People in Their Own Words.* London: Jessica Kingsley Publishers.

Strang, J.F., Knauss, M., van der Miesen, A., McGuire, J.K. *et al.* (2020) 'A clinical program for transgender and gender-diverse neurodiverse/autistic adolescents developed through community-based participatory design.' *Journal of Clinical Child & Adolescent Psychology*, 6, 1–16.

Strang, J.F., Powers, M.D. Knauss, M., Sibarium, E. *et al.* (2018) '"They thought it was an obsession": Trajectories and perspectives of autistic transgender and gender-diverse adolescents.' *Journal of Autism and Developmental Disorders*, 48(12), 4039–4055

Tikuna, J. & Lavinas Picq, M. (2019) 'Indigenous Sexualities: Resisting Conquest and Translation.' In C. Cottet & M. Lavinas Picq (eds), *Sexuality and Translation in World Politics.* E-International Relations.

Yergeau, M.R. (2020) 'Cassandra isn't doing the robot: On risky rhetorics and contagious autism.' *Rhetoric Society Quarterly*, 50(3), 212–221.

Yurcaba, J. (2021, 4 February) 'New York repeals "walking while trans" law after years of activism.' *NBC News*. Available at www.nbcnews.com/feature/nbc-out/new-york-repeals-walking-while-trans-law-after-years-activism-n1256736 [accessed 27 April 2021].

Part 2

WORKING at the Intersection of Autism and Trans and/or Non-Binary Experiences

Chapter 6

Implications for Practice at Gender Identity Clinics

WORKING WITH AUTISTIC TRANSGENDER AND NON-BINARY INDIVIDUALS

Isabelle Hénault

Introduction

For almost ten years, there has been an increase in the requests for sexology consultations in various clinics that specialize in autism. The concept of gender identity and expression is a central preoccupation for many adolescents and adults. Recent support guidelines for autistic individuals (Strang *et al.*, 2016) show how the current knowledge and approaches have been adapted for the autistic presentation.

Clinical experience and current literature make it possible to identify three types of requests and clinical follow-up:

1. An exploration of the flexibility of gender, which is common in autistic individuals, and/or the possibility of a confusion that lies in an underlying conflict.

2. Access to diagnostic testing (after a consultation at a gender clinic) for autistic individuals, which highlights a new perspective on experience and the search for gender identity in adults.

3. Support for autistic adults for medical and/or social gender transition.

These three themes will be illustrated using clinical cases and a literature review that supports different clinical hypotheses.

The purpose of this chapter is to help professionals navigate clinically to better support the specific needs of transgender and non-binary autistic individuals. Finally, it offers some educational approaches and tools.

1. Gender identity and how it is expressed in autistic individuals

An important component of sexuality links to gender identity. Clinical observations and discussions with a group of adults with a mixture of transgender, non-binary and atypical gender presentations (the authors did not distinguish among these groups at the time of publication) indicate the possibility of a correlation between being autistic and experiencing gender dysphoria (Israel and Tarver, 1997). Gender dysphoria refers to the feeling of not belonging to one's biological sex and its resulting body image. From the point of view of certain researchers and clinicians it is not a disorder but a fluid and diverse approach to gender.

Some data and research

Better understanding of gender identity and its diversity in autistic individuals requires further investigation. According to Williams, Allard and Sears (1996), there are three to ten times more cases of autistic individuals in gender identity clinics. These findings confirmed the impact of autism characteristics relating to gender identity. Having to understand themselves through neurotypical constructs and ideas may lead to an impaired view of themselves for some autistic people, and the absence of development of the concept of self-identity can lead to difficulties understanding one's own gender identity.

For Galluci, Hackerman and Schmidt (2005), neurodiverse socio-sexual development is one of the main factors to consider in autistic populations. In his research, he describes the case of a male in his forties who adopted feminine gender presentation at nine years old and masturbated for the first time at 29 years old. This type of development is rather rare in neurotypical populations and therefore confirms the importance of considering gender identity disorder in the sexual profile of autistic people (Hénault, 2005, 2019). Environmental factors, family systems, socialization, prenatal hormones and the neuronal density of the hypothalamus may all play a part (*Gale Encyclopaedia of Psychology*, 2001; Stonehouse, 2003).

Autism: a new perspective on gender identity

Gender fluidity is described as the combination of masculine and feminine characteristics in clothing, personality traits, activities and physical appearance. This fluidity is lived and expressed without inner conflict and many autistic individuals describe it as 'gender neutrality'. Both clinical experience and academic research (Davidson & Tamas, 2016; Jones *et al.*, 2011; Kourti & MacLeod, 2018) indicate that approximately 30–40 per cent of autistic individuals without learning difficulties may identify in this way. There are various noteworthy hypotheses that attempt to explain this, both in clinical settings and from the testimonies of autistic individuals.

To begin with, a personal exploration of gender identity which is not limited to conforming to social norms gives freedom for some autistic people. Thus, they integrate the richness and complexity of gender without social barriers or judgement of others, as was discussed in Chapters 2 and 4. As they are less receptive to social influence, they act authentically on their own experience. Furthermore, several autistic people often say that they don't understand why society dictates behaviours, attitudes and appearance when inside them there is this beautiful combination of masculine and feminine which is their wealth and it defines them in their uniqueness. Another factor often mentioned is that of gender neutrality, which is characterized by a rejection of genders. This is evident in the choice of clothing, the overall physical appearance (haircut, accessories, etc.) or through interests that are not bound by gender stereotypes. The person defines and expresses themselves through an apparent and harmonious neutrality.

In terms of this fluidity, it is possible to observe a continuum that is expressed by preferences (clothes typically assigned to the opposite sex or considered neutral), a spectrum that is showcased in a variety of gender expressions (often what might be considered 'opposite' gender expression, or a gender neutral one) and various stages of medical transition, such as hormone therapy and gender-affirming surgeries. In order to ensure adequate follow-up with these individuals, it is recommended to carry out an evaluation in order to understand their personal motivations and desired outcomes. To do so, the use of a questionnaire must be combined with the clinical experience of the professional. The Gender Identity Profile (Israel & Tarver, 1997) questionnaire is composed of 40 questions on imagi-nation, behaviour, gender expression, sexual behaviour, desired or undertaken transition steps (hormone therapy, electrolysis, surgery, etc.), desires and mental health problems (depression, anxiety, etc.). In a complementary document, Dr Israel (personal communication) has also added a series of questions relevant to autistic people. She is interested in the link between autism and gender dysphoria and recommends follow-up approaches for transgender individuals. The analysis of the questionnaire results allows the professional to identify whether the person is interested in transitioning socially or medically, and whether they are interested in gender neutrality/ flexibility rather than a permanent binary transition.

It is also important to consider the sexual development of some autistic people. Behavioural history often contributes to the de-velopment of socio-sexual skills and autistic people often develop those skills later in life compared to non-autistic people (Hénault, 2005). Autistic people often present a different developmental pathway from that of neurotypical people and are less likely to have sustained socio-sexual experiences and knowledge in the same time frames as their neurotypical peers. Furthermore, the exploration and questioning of identity may be expressed beyond puberty more often in autistic individuals. Contrary to the criteria established for the gender identity assessment (American Psychiatric Association 2012), it is not uncommon to meet autistic people who question and explore their identity towards the end of adolescence and adulthood. In our autism clinic, we tend to see more referrals for autistic adults because, generally speaking, they did not have the opportunity to speak with a professional until that point. This must not be a criterion for the exclusion of the possibility of gender diversity. This is what one young adult reported, during a discussion on their questionnaire: 'It seems to be necessary to choose between being a boy and being a girl or young woman. In my case, could I choose to be between the two?' This is very interesting; we were able to explore this possibility outside the pathological framework and help this young person come to terms with their own characteristics and experiences in order to consolidate their own personal, sexual and gender identity.

In their article 'Autism and the ghost of gender', Davidson and Tamas, (2016) discuss gender identity as a social construct. Based on first-hand accounts, online surveys, blogs, and the autobiographies of 75 autistic participants, the article concludes that gender as a construct is more abstract for autistic individuals. A majority of subjects won't comply to specific rules or a quest to relate to a binary gender model. Unlike neurotypical people who are compliant to strong social and educational models of male and female roles, autistic people do not conform to the same social roles. They view gender identity in a more personal way and as a broad journey. This social model is absolutely pertinent in explaining the perceptions of various adults who do not recognize themselves in the social roles linked with gender and gender identity. When the changes (in orientation or sexual behaviour) are drastic and sudden, they usually indicate a reaction to an event or condition. When sexual diversity is experienced over a significant period of time, it marks a difference more in terms of the individual, their personality and tastes.

Sometimes, neurotypical partners may report cross-dressing episodes from their autistic partner. The latter experiments with gender non-conforming and accessories in order to expand the couple's repertoire of sexual activities. Freed from taboos, they have fun with the concept of gender identity. It is also possible that a preference for gender non-conforming accessories or clothing is considered gender fluidity because it is not sexual fetishism but rather an attraction for a colour, textures, an appearance usually associated with the 'opposite' sex (sequins, dress, bow tie, hat, etc.). This mixed identification is common among autistic people who freely express their own appearance, without meeting social standards or criteria.

In addition, in terms of desire and sexual orientation, a woman in our self-help group 'Aspergirls' reported this: 'When I am attracted to someone sexually, it is the person who attracts me, regardless of their biological sex.' This was the start of long discussions about sexual orientation. About 30–40 per cent of autistic adults have also confirmed to me that for them the object of desire is not the male or female gender. This flexibility should not be taken in the sense of bisexuality but rather of pansexuality, which is characterized by physical, sexual or romantic attraction towards a person rather than a gender or sex.

Various movements of autistic adults claim this orientation in defence of their rights and their difference. Furthermore, a pioneer support group in the defines of the rights and the sexual expression of adults offers various services in California.¹ In his book, John D. Allen (2003) explores the various sexual expressions in people with different developmental conditions. It inspired me a lot in my research and clinical work, where meetings and exchanges with specialists from the Scandinavian countries made it possible to develop and structure better services for autistic people, in addition to training team professionals. Sexual desire and gender identity, which are two separate realities, should therefore not be confused. However, knowledge of these can promote a better understanding of gender fluidity, which is sometimes expressed through interpersonal or romantic relationships.

In cases where gender identity is conflicting with the gender the person was assigned at birth, it may be important to explore whether there are any other underlying unresolved issues that may affect an individual's desire to identify with the 'opposite' gender. For some, denial of the autism diagnosis is expressed by a desire for drastic change; by becoming a man or a woman (another person), they would no longer be autistic. This explanation was shared by many in consultation. For some, conflict can arise after the breakdown of a romantic relationship. Following rejection or disappointment, some people want a transformation, hoping to be more successful in their

---

1   http://centerforpg.com/rainbow-group.html

future relationships. Also, lack of sexual experience may precipitate a desire for change, which turns out to be of a conflictual nature. It may, therefore, be more of a choice based on perceived future benefits than a need to express their transgender or non-binary gender identity.

In some cases, gender issues become a special interest. Some autistic people develop a fascination that can appear as behaviours or attitudes that border on obsession, which is further discussed in Chapter 7. It is important, therefore, to make a differential assessment between the intense interest and the obsessive compulsive disorder (OCD). In general, interest leads to pleasure in understanding, researching and exchanging information on a subject, while OCD leads to intense anxiety. Before proposing an approach, the professional should explore the extent to which the anxiety present is a result of other underlying conditions, struggles with the social barriers that may come with wanting to transition medically or socially, gender dysphoria or some combination of all of these. The discomfort experienced by several people who want to undergo a gender transition can provoke intense emotions (anger, despair, fears, resentment), especially if they feel misunderstood or alone in this reality. It is essential, therefore, to provide support and information in order to clarify the process to help them make a decision.

If an autistic person feels intense and negative emotions around this area, several warnings are essential before proposing research on the internet. The professional and parents must provide recognized sites or access to a support system adapted for autistic people in order to avoid them ending up on unsuitable sites. For example, in our clinic we have a programme that allows autistic people to meet and discuss their experiences among themselves and we may also refer individuals to other gender identity clinics that offer group activities. We also refer people to other organizations like Autism Canada or other groups of autistic adults. Sometimes autistic people demonstrate a certain naivety, so the risk of them being exposed to intimidation or mistreatment is high. One young autistic woman said: 'As I feel bad and different from others, I told myself that I had to be trans. Following my research, I contacted a group on the internet, and they invited me to join their exchanges and activity.

Unfortunately, I discovered that their intentions were not the same as mine and it ended very badly.' By talking with her, we were able to find a support group which allowed her to progress positively, in addition to expanding her social circle.

Finally, the conflict can also arise due to difficulties linked to self-identity. An autistic woman explained to me 'Since I do not feel like the others and that I cannot find my place, I must be a man.' This very important aspect must be taken seriously in order to support adolescents and adults who experience the social stigma of being autistic, and although it can co-exist with being transgender, it doesn't necessarily. To avoid distress, it is recommended that a professional follows the guidelines (Strang *et al.*, 2016) and provides adequate follow-up. The role of the professional is to provide sympathetic support and facilitate access to adapted services. If a conflict is the source, the professional should focus on strategies to help consolidate, accept and live well with this difference before addressing the problem of gender identity, which may be an indication of other challenges, not a solution. If the desire to pursue gender transition is real and motivated, the procedures must consider the autistic profile, as mentioned in the guidelines of Strang *et al.* (2016).

These are guidelines for clinical approaches that should be prioritized, according to the authors' clinical experiences:

- Autistic adolescents may have limited self-awareness and may struggle to recognize or understand their gender concerns until later in development.

- Rigid, overly concrete thinking (black-and-white thinking) may lead to an impulsive decision.

- Adolescents who are clearly in an exploratory phase of gender should be encouraged to explore their gender identity over time before being considered for medical treatments. At the end of this chapter, there are some suggestions for approaches and tools that might be helpful in supporting young people and allowing them to explore the different stages of gender identity, in order to make an informed choice.

- Many young autistic people are socially isolated and it's important to provide positive social experiences through group activities. It also increases the self-esteem through feedback from other group members.

- Young people with this co-occurrence may have difficulty following a specific medical protocol due to executive function impairments, which often remain unaddressed. Coaching-type support will allow for the establishment of a sequence of steps to be taken and scheduled meetings. Without falling into over-protection, it is a good idea to use effective visual organization tools (tables, diary, sequences on computer/iPad, etc). We recommend taking the Behavior Rating Inventory of Executive Function (BRIEF) (Gioia *et al.*, 2013) in order to explore the profile of executive functions and dysfunctions, such as mental flexibility, impulsiveness, organization, notion of time, priorities and sequences. Analysis of the profile then makes it possible to establish practical and effective recommendations in order to increase organizational skills.

- There is a high risk of victimization. The social aspects of being autistic in a neurotypical world can be very taxing for these people, so we need to encourage assertiveness. Access to a virtual support/education group adapted for autistic people is a way of fostering acceptance and friendship, which acts as a protective factor. The group's social influence also makes it possible to join in a welcoming environment and thus allows social exchanges, discussions and the sharing of personal experiences.

2. Access to the diagnostic assessment for autism

Several adolescents and adults come to our clinic for a consultation for a diagnostic evaluation. Following the tests, a clinical interview explores the characteristics and behaviours associated with autism. Also, various subjects are approached in connection with the developmental history and the concept of personal identity and gender spontaneously. Many describe a feeling of difference from neurotypical family members and the peer group. For some, the quest for identity and the feeling of belonging may develop later, towards the beginning of adulthood. For others, the sense of difference initially associated with autism reveals another level of difference associated with gender identity. The autism diagnosis then highlights the stages of psychosexual development which, in some cases, may explain a fluid gender identity. For example, during the diagnostic assessment, one 20-year-old individual who was assigned female at birth reported feeling different from other adults their age. They talked about their interests in history, literature, manga, and the discrepancy they observed in terms of their social behaviour. Often in the background, they observed many others in order to decode their gestures, attitudes and ways of relating. They listed the friendly and romantic attempts that never materialized. In discussing their feeling of masculinity, they evoked memories of childhood during family vacations where the boys and girls played independently:

> I never really knew which group to play with. I loved Lego building games as much as forest walks where I explored insects and butterflies. On the way back, I could draw for hours with my sisters (butterflies, castles, imaginary world) without getting tired. Later, the pressure from the peer group was difficult for me because I was somehow asked to choose between boys' and girls' games when for me there had never been any difference. In fact, I was neither a boy nor a girl myself. I liked to dress in bright colours reminiscent of those of the forest, butterflies, flowers... I never imagined that we had to follow 'codes'. I was suddenly reminded of this when I was a teenager and the grey and black uniform was made compulsory. However, I would have liked so much to be able to wear colourful and flowing clothes because for me, it had nothing to do with the image of masculinity or femininity so coveted by my peers. Later, I was asked about my attractions because it seems that I had not clearly indicated my preferences...but why choose between genders when it is the person who interests me. My friends are my friends, regardless of their gender; it is the same for my attraction.

Following the assessment that confirmed a diagnosis of autism spectrum disorder level 1 (formerly known as Asperger syndrome), we continued the discussion about their identity. They felt a pressure to have to choose and explained that for them, this duality was natural. We were able to explore the different layers of their identity (see the sexual systems exercise presented later in the chapter) in order to consolidate their identity core and promote the expression of their sexuality, preferences, gender identity and eroticism. This clinical work allowed a positive journey towards self-understanding and acceptance without having to choose a gender. Believing that they should one day formally identify as a man or a woman, they felt significant and compelling anxiety. By integrating the idea and the feeling that they could choose to be neutral, non-binary, to choose themself, a whole weight just fell away. Several similar cases have been reported in the literature and in the clinic.

Access to an autism diagnosis can therefore shed light on the person's gender neutrality, duality or fluidity. Moreover, this information should be considered during the support in order to properly guide the future choices of autistic people.

The transition to puberty is also an important step to consider in young autistic people. The many body and genital changes can cause anxiety because these changes are experienced outside the person's control. This is a time of transition. For example, breast growth can cause different reactions in young autistic girls. As this change is visible, a number of young girls will rejoice at the transformation as it is a sign of feminization. Having breasts reassures the girl of her gender identity (her belonging to the female sex). Some young girls value femininity and feminine gender expression (clothing, makeup, hair, accessories, etc.). Other young girls fear puberty and the bodily transformations that accompany it. Breast growth can cause anxiety and, at the same time, difficulties because the changes materialize as part of one's secondary sex characteristics. This can become a defining moment in the process of gender identity and the desired transformations (hormone therapy, neutral and loose clothing, etc.), which is why we need to explore the concept of puberty with our young autistic people to make sure they have all the information and support they need. Another factor to consider is sensory sensitivities. Most autistic people can be hypersensitive or hyposensitive regarding some of their senses; hearing: smell, touch, sight, taste, kinesthesis, proprioception, and balance (Bogdashina, 2003; Côté, 2016). In addition, a sense often acts as a benchmark in relation to the others, by being more developed.

Hypersensitivity can be understood as an extreme sensitivity in one or various senses of an individual. Regarding sexual and gender identity, the five senses – hearing, smell, touch, taste, and sight –are very important. In autistic people without learning difficulties, hearing and tactile hypersensitivity are very present and may be associated with a neurological difference (Bogdashina, 2003). For example, ambient music may be perceived as shrill and loud, while the volume is at a low level – just as a touch on the skin can cause the same pain as that felt by contact with a sharp object. In terms of sexuality, over-sensitivity can hinder the establishment of an intimate relationship because the various stimulations then cause discomfort, even pain. Avoiding contact can increase feelings of isolation and amplify depressive symptoms. Alternatively, the skin pressure (sometimes deep) is often perceived as calming (Aquilla, 2003).

On the other hand, hyposensitivity is defined as a weak sensory response to stimuli felt to be weak. In this case, an over-exposure to stimuli is necessary so that the individual can feel them fully. Aquilla (2003) explains these reactions as a slow process of the transfer of sensations between the nerve endings of the skin and the brain. In their book, *In the Autistic Brain*, Temple Grandin and Richard Panek (2013) put forward an interesting hypothesis that hypersensitivity and hyposensitivity may have a common origin, which is basically hypersensitivity. It is sensory overload that causes hyposensitivity, as a kind of protection.

For some autistic people, genital sensitivity can become a hindrance. A negative genital feeling (uncomfortable/painful) can lead to an aversion to that area of the body. In some cases, the desire for surgery may be linked to the feeling of being released from the physical genital sensation. To avoid dramatic situations related to impulsivity, it is important to ask questions about genital mutilation behaviours. If they are present, it is imperative to offer sensory

(Bogdashina, 2003) and sexological help. It is important to understand whether the difficulties the individual faces are because of gender dysphoria, or aversion to their genital organs. If it is an aversion, it is usually targeted at the genitals, whereas gender dysphoria tends to be more generalized. By exploring their sensory profile, genital discomfort and the possibility of aversion, we can target the difficulties and offer adapted strategies.

In some autistic women, vaginal penetration is experienced painfully, due to tactile hypersensitivity. This pain is comparable to that experienced by women who develop vulvar vestibulitis syndrome (VVS). Symptoms such as burning or warming of the vaginal entrance are described. The treatment of VVS includes certain preventive elements which aim to restore the balance of the vaginal flora and so avoid irritation or infections in women who demonstrate sensitivity. Thus, it becomes possible to separate the sensory (and sexual) factors from a desire for change, which becomes a solution to a difficulty associated with autism spectrum disorder. All the work that relates to body image is also important in order to find suitable solutions. A tool is presented in the proposed approaches section.

3. The pathways to support adults in transition: approaches and adapted tools

Several approaches encourage the exploration of gender identity in order to consolidate the positive feelings associated with the person's own identity. Professionals can therefore offer tools and support adolescents and adults. A first step is to develop the person's social and interpersonal skills in order to widen their circle of knowledge, friendships and mutual support. One of the components concerns the stages of relationships, the limits, the appropriate interactions, and the components of romantic and sexual relationships. The goal is to foster security and avoid intimidation or social isolation. Various programmes and books tackle these themes using situations and structured educational cards that allow effective learning adapted for autistic people. (Edmonds & Worton, 2005; Hénault, 2005; Organization for Autism Research, 2019; Ramey & Ramey, 2008; Stanford, 2013).

The 'Circles' exercise allows you to explore the five major components linked to identity – body, self, sexuality, social ties and romantic relationships, and autism - in a visual way. Each circle is presented and discussed using concrete examples (photos, videos, script) to ensure that the 'ingredients' that make up a coherent whole are understood. This allows both the professional and the autistic person to address the facets of identity and to identify whether certain components appear problematic or related to a conflict. The representation in the form of circles is inclusive and personal to everyone. Once addressed, the components form a whole that will be coherent (flexibility, fluidity, neutrality, 'autigen' or autistic gender identity). If one or more spheres are problematic, this demonstrates the presence of a conflict which will then be targeted by our approaches (e.g. social skills, isolation, amorous disappointments, restrictive sensory sensitivities, dislike of private parts). This will not prevent the choice or the transition decision, but the support will aim to prioritize the difficulties before approaching future choices. Also, this allows you to take the time necessary for personal work and reflections in the event that the transition becomes an obsession (Strang *et al.*, 2016).

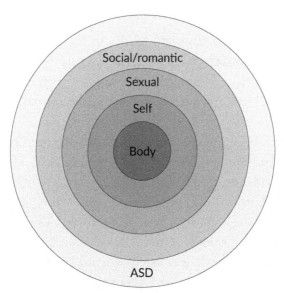

Circles of identity

Another step concerns the *'sensory profile'*. By presenting images and photos of whole bodies, the professional will be able to address sensory sensitivities and the perception of the body of the autistic person. Through neutral and educational material, emotions will be sidelined for the benefit of a logical and factual exchange. This strategy promotes the sharing of information on general and intimate parts of the body. Sexual function is then approached (erection, ejaculation, vaginal lubrication, swelling of the clitoris, etc.), then reproduction and, finally, the image of the body. By using neutral images, it is then easier for the autistic person to approach their own body image, sensory sensitivities and sexual reactions, as is also discussed in Chapters 7 and 9. In detail, the whole body can be discussed (both male and female) in order to access bodily thoughts, representations and feelings. An open discussion thus promotes access to useful information that will guide the next steps in the approach. Here again, the verbal and non-verbal exchanges will give clues to the congruence or incongruence of the body, the profile of sensitivities and the desired changes, if this is the case.

The theory of sexual systems (Rubio, 1998) composes an explanatory grid of sexuality and gender. The individual is at the centre and expresses himself through his gender, his eroticism, his body, and his emotional relationships. The professional then guides the discussion by following the stages and associated themes in order to explore the knowledge and experiences of the autistic person. This tool allows you to address the relevant questions, related to the construction of self and identity. For example, past painful experiences or abuse are sometimes a precipitating factor in the conflict. Social isolation or lack of relationship or love experiences can be central to the desire for transition. The objective is to explore the sub-themes in an educational and neutral way to help the person understand and clarify (if a conflict is present) the components linked to gender identity. When it comes to flexibility, the exercise will be just as interesting as it allows you to explore in detail the representation and personal experience of the autistic person through its four components.

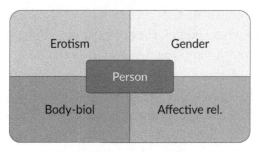

Holones sexuales
(Eusebio Rubio, 1998)

In a completely different matter, if the autistic person experiences difficulties related to executive functions, the results of the BRIEF test (Gioia *et al.*, 2015) will highlight the strategies to be developed. The book *Flexible and Focused* (Najdowski 2017) contains several concrete examples that improve organization, planning, cognitive flexibility and the concept of time.

Conclusion

The theme of gender identity is complex and so rich that it is impossible to fully understand and describe it. In addition, each autistic person is unique. The objective of this chapter was to provide a summary or clinical portrait of the hypotheses and observations arising from consultations over the years. Fortunately, research studies and publications on the subject are becoming more numerous and allow us to enrich our knowledge and approaches. We have yet to fully disentangle and understand gender identity in autistic people. The practitioner must remain cautious in their conclusions in order to support people positively. They must adopt an approach centred on the individual, not pathologizing but being respectful of the very nature of autistic people.

Body	• Preception • Sensory aspects	
Gender	• Identity • Dysphoria • Flexibility or conflict	
Eroticism	• Paraphilia • Abuse • Harassment	Sexual dysfunction Homophobia
Affective	• **Violence** • Immaturity • Experiences	• **Relationships** • Private–Public • Intimacy

Holones sexuales

References

Allen, J.D. (2003) *Gay, Lesbian, Bisexual, and Transgender People with Developmental Disabilities and Mental Retardation: Stories of the Rainbow Support Group.* London: Routledge.

American Psychiatric Association (2012) *Diagnostic and Statistical Manual of Mental Disorders* (4th ed.: DSM-IV). Washington, DC: American Psychiatric Association.

Aquilla, P. (2003) 'Sensory issues in individuals with Asperger Syndrome.' *The Second National Conference on Asperger's Syndrome.* Toronto: Aspergers Society of Ontario.

Bogdashina, O. (2003) *Sensory Perceptual Issues in Autism and Asperger Syndrome: Different Sensory Experiences – Different Perceptual Worlds.* London: Jessica Kingsley Publishers.

Côté, S. (2016) *Favoriser l'Attention par des Stratégies Sensorielles.* Montréal: Chenelière Education.

Davidson, J. & Tamas, S. (2016) 'Autism and the ghost of gender.' *Emotion, Space and Society,* 19: 59–65.

Edmonds, G. & Worton, D. (2005) *The Asperger Love Guide.* London: Paul Chapman Publishing.

Gale Encyclopedia of Psychology (2001) *Gender Identity Disorder* (2nd ed.) Farmington, MI: Gale Group.

Gallucci, G., Hackerman, F. & Schmidt, C.W. (2005) 'Gender identity disorder in an adult male with Asperger's syndrome.' *Sexuality and Disability,* 23(1), 35–40.

Gioia, G., Isquith, P., Guy, S. & Kenworthy, L. (2015) *Behavior Rating Inventory of Executive Function (BRIEF).* Available at www.parinc.com/Products/Pkey/25 [accessed 27 April 2021].

Grandin, T. & Panek, R. (2013) *The Autistic Brain.* Boston, MA: Houghton Mifflin Harcourt.

Hénault, I. (2005) *Asperger Syndrome and Sexuality*. London: Jessica Kingsley Publishers.

Israel, G.E. & Tarver, D.E. (1997) *Transgender Care*. Philadelphia, PA: Temple University Press.

Jones, S., Wheelwright, K., Farrell, E., Martin, R. *et al.* (2011) 'Brief report: Female-to-male transsexual people and autistic traits.' *Journal of Autism and Developmental Disorders*, 42(2), 301–306.

Kourti, M. & MacLeod, A. (2018) 'I don't feel like a gender, I feel like myself: Autistic individuals raised as girls exploring gender identity.' *Autism in Adulthood*, 1, 1.

Najdowski, A.C. (2017) *Flexible and Focused*. Academic Press.

Organization for Autism Research (2019) Sex ed for self-advocates. Available at https://researchautism.org/sex-ed-guide [accessed 27 April 2021].

Ramey, E.M. & Ramey, J.J. (2008) *Autistics' Guide to Dating: A Book by Autistics, for Autistics and Those Who Love Them or Who Are in Love with Them*. London: Jessica Kingsley Publishers.

Rubio, E. (1998) *Holones sexuales*. AMSSAC Asociacion. Mexico.

Stanford, A. (2013) *Troubleshooting Relationships on the Autism Spectrum: A User's Guide to Resolving Relationship Problems*. London: Jessica Kingsley Publishers.

Stonehouse, M. (2003) *Gender Identity Conflicts on the Autistic Spectrum and the Possible Co-Morbidity Between Them*. Toronto: Canadian-American Research Consortium on Autistic Spectrum Disorders.

Strang, J.F., Meagher, H., Kenworthy, L., de Vries, A.L.C. *et al.* (2016) 'Initial clinical guidelines for co-occurring autism spectrum disorder and gender dysphoria or incongruence in adolescents.' *Journal of Clinical Child & Adolescent Psychology*, 47(1), 105–115.

Williams, P.G., Allard, A.M. & Sears, L. (1996) 'Case study: Cross-gender preoccupations in two male children with autism.' *Journal of Autism and Developmental Disorders*, 26(6), 635–642.

Chapter 7

Reflections on the Spectra of Autism and Gender Identity

CONSIDERATIONS FOR PROFESSIONALS SUPPORTING AUTISTIC TRANSGENDER AND NON-BINARY PEOPLE

Wenn Lawson

Introduction

This chapter briefly addresses issues related to building an understanding of autism and gender as individual spectra of experience. Knowing oneself and one's gender identity is different for us all. However, uncovering this reality can be a delayed experience for many on the autism spectrum. Research suggests that there are connections between gender identity and the autistic population that are perhaps stronger than those with the non-autistic population (Dattaro, 2020; Saleh, 2014).

This chapter asks what it could mean if there are connections, why these connections might exist, and what they might mean for professionals supporting autistic individuals with gender identity differences. This is important because fear of mistakes may immobilize professionals and render them ineffective in this arena. This chapter offers suggestions and ideas which might be useful in addressing some of these fears. It also explores ways to support autistic individuals on their journey of self-discovery, particularly regarding their gender identities. To help with the latter, this chapter addresses concepts associated with interoception and object permanence – two areas often active but possibly 'offline' in autism – and encourages professionals to listen to the stories of those they support.

As a trans masculine autistic adult who is also a certified psychologist, a registered social worker, a husband/parent to autistic offspring and grandparent to autistic grandchildren, I am committed to understanding and supporting autistic individuals. My work as a researcher with universities in the UK and Australia has led to exploring why anxiety is so high within the autistic and gender-diverse population. Some of the reasoning may seem obvious: autism means lots of differences, often not understood by professionals supporting autistic people. However, there are also areas of autistic experience that have, seemingly, 'flown under the radar'. I want to start a conversation about these and highlight their existence.

Connections between gender dysphoria and autism

To date, there is little research on autism and gender identity to help us understand what inter-relationship, if any, they may share. However, as we listen to adults tell their stories, maybe we will get some clues. The incidence of gender dysphoria appears to be higher in the adult autistic population, or those adults with autistic characteristics, higher by 6–7 per cent (Heylens *et al.*, 2018) when compared to 1 per cent of the non-autistic population. But this does not necessitate a 'true' correlation so much as it shows that the experience of gender variance is more common in autistic people and the journey of self-discovery will vary from that of the non-autistic population.

As autistic people, we are usually honest individuals not necessarily concerned with social norms and expectations, unless they are those of shared values. It makes sense, therefore, that gender discrepancies might follow, as it was explored in Chapter 4. If you value equally an individual for who they are, no matter their gender, you might be equally at home in either gender. But if your biology is at odds with your assigned gender, you might be more connected (eventually) to your 'brain'-disposed gender rather than your physical gender. Currently, we just do not know which comes first (if either does), the chicken or the egg. In many ways, maybe it is not as important to know as it is to recognize where an individual is on their journey and support them with what they need at that time.

For example, an individual may feel uncomfortable with their currently identified gender (gender assigned at birth) but not know what this means for them. Having a professional commit to taking the journey with them and exploring what this might mean is so important. It starts with listening, without judgement. They may need support to move beyond that discomfort and explore their brain and interoceptive connection (what it is their mind and deeper senses are saying). For example, feelings of attraction to women's clothing may be a sensory, calming thing, not connected to sexuality or gender. It may also be a feeling of disconnection to living in a gendered body, or a need based in sexual desire, a combination of the above or something else entirely, as was also discussed in Chapter 6. Being 'joined' up enough to tell the difference isn't always easy in autism, especially combined with the stigma that being autistic and gender variant carry as well as the inadequate and sparse amount of information about this intersection. However, there are also autistic people who are insistent on their need for recognition of being transgender because they 'always knew' and they need to explore the whole concept of social and medical transition – and there are many and various places in between.

Statistics

We know that gender and sexuality lie along a spectrum of varying experience and may be more fluid than set, especially in autistic people. However, the previously mentioned 6–7 per cent may be a conservative estimate. In one narrative review, researchers reported: 'As up to around 20% of gender identity clinic-assessed individuals reported clinical range features of ASD, we can cautiously conclude that co-occurring GD [gender dysphoria] and ASD is frequent' (van der Miesen, Hurley & de Vries, 2016, p.78).

Mental health in both populations (autistic and gender questioning; those with gender dysphoria and the transgender population) is said to be poor in general, and coupled together could produce some concerning statistics. For example, some small studies suggest alarming suicide rates in the transgender population: 'a staggering 41% of transgender people have attempted to commit suicide compared to 5% of the general population' (Williams, 2017). It is also suggested that a further 10 per cent of autistic teens attempt suicide above the rate usual in the non-autistic population.

The impact of being autistic in a non-accepting society, not having access to appropriate support, experiencing societal scorn, gaps in resources and a lack of role models, all appear to contribute to the statistics above. It is, therefore, very important to listen to our stories, to learn how to respond and support us appropriately.

In autistic people, it is also imperative to know whether gender discomforts are related to sensory connections or to gender identity. Being open, with appropriate support, to exploring these issues may reduce many of the mental health difficulties we experience. For example, does the discomfort with menstruation (pretending it is not happening; refusing to wear a pad or tampon; refusing to acknowledge puberty challenges) reflect a distressed sensory system or is it a sign of gender dysphoria? It is important to listen to the wider story an individual is telling us. If the discomfort is part of a bigger picture (for example, it accompanies a dislike of all things female, such as clothing, hobbies, expectations, and the person is saying things like 'I am a boy'), we can usually explore the issue as a gender concern rather than a sensory one. I know that this isn't always the case, however, especially when one's interoception (internal sensory system) is not connecting to an appropriate sense. For example, as an autistic adult I still can't tell the difference between feeling hungry and being thirsty. Sometimes I try to satisfy one of these, only to realize it's the other that needs attention! For me, as an autistic person, this has meant a very long journey to connect the pieces of the puzzle (my life and gender) so I understand what my gender identity is, separate to my sensory differences and my sexual orientation.

Male brain in autism

Some might argue that autism means having a more masculinized brain, due to more testosterone in utero, and that this explains the higher statistics for gender dysphoria in autistic females (Baron-Cohen, 1999). Although there is some evidence that autistic females may have a more extreme male brain (EMB), which is still debated, there is also no evidence that the same is true for autistic males (Lai *et al.*, 2013). So, however you look at it, EMB theory does not explain gender dysphoria or autism, especially considering that autistic trans women are not at all considered by this approach, which is further discussed in Chapter 11. In fact, there is some research to suggest that if we looked at the brains of trans women (identified male at birth) their brains would more likely resemble those of cis women (cis = birth identified gender, the one a person is living in) and the opposite is true for trans men identified as female at birth (e.g. Bakker, 2018; Reardon, 2019; Williams, 2018).

When it comes to issues of gender dysphoria and subsequent transition from gender assigned at birth to the gender one is more at home with, it appears the literature is still unclear whether one gender is more likely than another to experience gender dysphoria (Murphy *et al.*, 2020). However, trans women are more visible in the media, whereas trans men may 'pass' more unnoticed. This might be because it is more usual for women to wear male clothing than for men to wear female clothing. Furthermore, it may be less complicated and less 'dangerous' for a female to pass as male than for a male to pass as female because femininity is far more policed than masculinity. So, although this makes trans women more visible, the numbers in the trans population are probably equal (Leinung & Jalaja, 2019). Maybe because as autistic people we are not so bound by social rules of needing to conform and are freer to be ourselves, there appear to be more trans people in our population. As for genetics and the role of hormones in issues of gender, there is no evidence either way that gender dysphoria, being more prominent in autism, is due solely to this. However, the research is in its infancy and there is much to explore. For me, the reasons are not as important as the need to have our stories heard and for the right support to be available for the individual.

Assessment

Appropriate support, as assessment is explored, cannot be overestimated. Having family, friends and colleagues take us seriously may begin with professional identification. I was once told that as I pursued my assessment for gender dysphoria and then followed through with actions to help me move beyond it, I might lose my autism diagnosis. The psychiatrist I saw said this had happened to some of his 'patients'. He believed that gender dysphoria and autism closely mirrored one another, often disguising one or more mental health issues. It made me uncomfortable to think of this, as alleviating suffering and getting the right assessment for the right condition should be uppermost in the mind of the professional. Of course, many autistic people live with co-occurring conditions, as does the rest of humanity. For example, I am autistic but also live with attention deficit hyperactivity disorder (ADHD), specific learning disorder (previously known as dyslexia and dyscalculia) and dyspraxia, and I have issues with auditory processing plus visual impairment (mostly remedied with prescription lenses). Being human opens a door to all manner of issues, some hidden, others more evident. It's part of neurodiversity, which means we are all living with diversity and difference in our brains and neurology. Judy Singer defines neurodiversity along similar lines to biodiversity. It just means we all have brains that think, learn, reason and relate differently (personal conversation, 2021); it's part of being human!

For this chapter, the elements that need considering, despite their overlap, are the issues specific to gender identity in autism. It may be possible that not feeling connected to who you are may have to do with poor interoception, poor object permanence, and an autistic disposition causing delay and disconnection and/or contributing to gender dysphoria, as it is later explored in this chapter. Teasing these out as you get to know an individual, separating the broader sensory world and that of attention issues in autism will all help to construct evidence either way. It is a bit like deducing the reason and impact of a behaviour by noting what is missing and what is existing, why and what it all means. Understanding these things also helps with anxieties around correctly assessing and diagnosing an autistic person with gender dysphoria, which may be a worry for professionals.

Fear of making a mistake

As professionals, we might be so worried about making a mistake or upsetting the status quo that we postpone making a firm diagnosis. This fear is partly based on the incorrect assumption that it is better, or even possible, for adults to make decisions on behalf of children and adolescents 'for their own good', as discussed in Chapter 3. Yet, if as professionals we are to 'do no harm' and if we take our clients seriously, we should be listening to their stories and acting accordingly. One way to support autistic younger people is to be ready to give hormone blockers. Giving a child nearing puberty puberty-blocking hormones simply delays puberty, giving the child (family and professional) more time to sort things out. For a boy who says they are a girl, allowing them to go through puberty, have their voice deepen and grow taller – well, there is no coming back from this. However, postponing these events, while doing no harm, buys everyone time. Research shows that if children reach adolescence while still insisting that they are transgender, 95–99 per cent will continue in their chosen gender as adults (Guerra *et al.*, 2020; Davies *et al.*, 2019; Wiepjes *et al.*, 2018). This is very high.

What if a young person changes their mind? After all, it does happen. Those who detransition have their own story. Sometimes it is only by going through a door that you discover it to be the wrong one. Maybe that path led to finding the one that was right, further down the track. Who are we to judge? This type of fear should not prevent us from listening to the stories we are being told now. Also, temporarily detransitioning can be part of an individual's journey along the way to a more permanent transition. For example, if social pressures are preventing an individual from continuing to explore their gender (they fear losing employment, losing a relationship or losing family support), they may put their transition on hold. However, the potential mental trauma from this could push an individual into further anxiety, depression and suicidality. For some, exploring why they are not comfortable with their gender assigned at birth leads them to conclude they are non-binary. This gender non-conformity arises from a knowledge the individual is not static in their gender but at home with a sense of 'they/them' rather than male or female.

The version of detransitioning that is mostly portrayed by the media and gender critical perspectives is, therefore, only a very small portion of an already very small group of people.

Our stories

In my experience and in sharing stories with other older autistic people, autism is one more window through which the above aspects impact to influence social and biological connectivity. This means that despite gender being both 'hardwired' within the brain and impacted by social expectations (Sanbonmatsu, 2019), in autism, connections to knowing who we are and processing this information may not be as developmentally formed as they are for the non-autistic population, (i.e. they may be delayed). 'Trans people with autism express a gender at odds with societal expectations or reject the male–female divide entirely. Many are breaking new ground on how identity is defined – and what it means to also have autism' (Rudacille, 2016).

Interoception

Interoception, sometimes called the eighth sense (after the vestibular and proprioceptive senses), lets us know when we are tired, hungry, thirsty, sexually aroused, hot, cold, anxious, angry, in pain, and so on. In autism, it is often naturally offline, not necessarily an appropriately connected experience. For example, an autistic individual may not pick up on the signals of thirst, hunger or anxiety; they may simply know they are uncomfortable (Goodall, 2016). Yet, without connection to this very important sense, gender identity may be less well established. Autism, by its very nature, implies the ability to make connections or notice elements of 'self' and of other people and things may be less available than in the population of non-autistic adults (unless this is an interest of focus). The literature demonstrates that shifting attention in autism can be very difficult, and problems with this and the ability to divide attention between senses, experiences, people and so on, is a core feature of autism (American Psychiatric Association, 2013; Lawson, 2011; Murray, Lesser & Lawson, 2005). Therefore, connecting to the interoceptive sense, which may be offline, is an important skill to develop in autistic people and will need particular attention.

For example, there are specific exercises that can help build and connect to our eighth sense and they can mean the difference between 'self-awareness' or not, and may contribute to the difference between connection to one's gender identity, or not. The Australian Department of Education has released some such exercises that may be of use to professionals working with autistic people (Goodall, 2019). Although these are illustrated for children, adapting them for adults is an easy task because the reasoning is the same. As we practice noticing where we feel 'the stretch', and so on, in our body, we are building cognitive connection, and this helps with 'noticing' what we are feeling in general. This is an important factor in noticing anxiety. If we don't recognize that our heart rate is increasing, our 'insides' feel tight, we can't do anything about it. Over time, autistic people can experience meltdowns, burnouts and/or shutdowns because the reactions are happening to them, whether or not they notice them or can label them. Consequently, they can go (seemingly) from 0–10 in their reactions, which come across as incredibly sudden and unpredictable to those around them. What happens in these cases is that the individual is not connecting to what they are feeling and suddenly their body cannot cope any more. Anxiety in autism is massive, and self-regulation is often unavailable simply because the autistic person doesn't know what they are feeling.

Of course, this does not mean that once interoception gets connected and experienced, this will lead to a more binary gender. It means that one's sense of self can be given the best chance to grow strong and individuals can gain better access to self-regulation, self-control, and self-acceptance, no matter what that ends up looking like. More discussion of the concept of interoception (and alexithymia) can be found in Chapter 9.

Object permanence

Object permanence (OP), or the sense that objects (and people and emotions) can still exist even when out of sight, is also often not an established cognitive awareness in autistic people. Autism is experienced as a developmental delay, and poorly formed or underdeveloped OP can be part of this package. This is an important understanding because it impacts gender identity too. Knowing that something, someone, an emotive state, a place and so on can still exist, even when unseen, is imperative for coping with change and daily transition.

It is likely that poor OP adds to some of the confusion in overlap between autism and gender incongruence. For example, most individuals have a 'sense' of who they are: male, female, non-binary and so on. But it can take time to feel at home with one's gender. It's not a case of 'being female means liking the colour pink and playing with dolls and eventually growing up into a woman who wants to marry a man and have children'. We know that gender is a spectrum experience and being female might mean a love of the colour green, playing football, wanting a single career, not having children and loving reality TV shows. In other words, the gender spectrum is broad, need not rely on gender stereotypes, and good self-esteem contributes to being comfortable with our own personal expression of who we are. But in whatever capacity we experience our gender, we need to have a concept for it. We need to be able to imagine or conjure up a picture (whether visual or not) of where we fit and belong. This knowledge can be thought of as a schema. Schemata, or maps of cognitive understanding, need connection and for that to happen we need to understand our feelings, our thoughts, and the intentions of self and of 'other'.

I stress this point because autistic individuals may find it difficult to identify emotions of self and others, and have difficulties in generalizing concepts or interpreting context. Sometimes they know they are feeling 'something', but they might not have the words for that feeling. Concepts and context require divided attention and connection from self to other. Difficulties in these areas can be misinterpreted as poor theory of mind, which is a neurotypically led, outdated approach, as discussed in Chapter 2. However, both OP (the knowing that objects, people, emotions continue to exist even when out of sight), and interoception (one's inner senses such as temperature and hunger) require a person to attend to multiple stimuli in order to appreciate concepts such as presence, absence, unseen presence, hunger, comfort, discomfort and so on.

This cognitive and sensory awareness impacts gender experience too. For example, for a very long time I knew I wasn't comfortable being 'female' no matter how hard I tried. I was told I was a 'tomboy' or a girl who liked what was considered more traditionally 'boyish things' (climbing trees, wearing masculine clothing, at home with rough and tumble play, preferring toy cars to dolls and loving to play football with the boys). I accepted that notion and eventually, when I was attracted sexually to females, I thought I must be lesbian. However, these ideas didn't feel right. I was uncomfortable with them, but I had no language or concepts to think differently. I decided I must be 'middle-sex' or be of a gender that wasn't traditionally female or male (I had a female body, so I did not think it possible to be male). This terminology still didn't give me a map or understanding of why I felt so drawn to masculine things though.

When the understanding and awareness of both OP and interoception improve, well-being and self-regulation are directly benefited. Giving individuals access to concepts, (the scheme of things) means building OP as a deliberate activity. It happens more easily to individuals who have brains wired to multi-task across areas, even when not interested (Lawson, 2011; Lawson & Dombroscki, 2017; Murray, Lesser & Lawson, 2005).

Autistic people often struggle with paying attention to several things simultaneously. This is one reason why the *DSM-5* (American Psychiatric Association, 2013) names two criteria for autism based on single attention (social and communication domain, and restrictive and repetitive interests and behaviours domain). Autistic individuals may not discern the fuller context of OP, and if interoception is not noted, gender connection may not be either. For example, autistic children might know their drink bottles are in their lunch bag, even when they can't see them, but they don't seem to know that Mummy is still Mummy if she has her hair cut or wears different clothes. Some autistic children call every man they see 'Daddy' because the unique qualities that differentiate one man from another are not noticed.

They still exist whether noticed or not, but if we don't 'note' these we will not connect to them. I was once asked for advice by a parent whose daughter loved to paint nail polish on her toenails. But, when she did this, she refused to wear shoes when going out. I suggested she might wear shoes if they had open 'toes' like sandals might. Then her daughter could see that the nail polish on the toenails were still there.

If OP and interoception are not well established in an autistic person, this needs rectifying. It's just one more tool in our toolkit that helps us deal with gender incongruence so we can get on with the work of discovering our true gender. However, if gender dysphoria continues despite good interoception and established OP, we need to look further. It may not relate to continued bodily understanding that is in line with the body's gender characteristics or to exploration of sensory differences; instead we may be uncovering gender dysphoria but still need support to see what this might mean for us.

Obsession?

In autistic people, special interests and obsessions (I prefer to call these passions) point to far deeper possibilities and can be lifetime events. As trans-individuals, we will show a passionate disposition towards our belief. Gender dysphoria is all consuming! Walking with us, without judgement, is the way forward. Laying all the cards on the table, saying it as it is and spelling it out for us is very helpful. Are my feelings connected to sensory discomforts or are they gender issues? If this is gender dysphoria and I transition, what might I experience? The outcomes that occur during transition may cause other discomforts. This information needs to be highlighted. For example, once I knew for sure and was on my transition journey, I found it overwhelming coping with the change of smell my body gave off as a male, compared to when I was female. Once I understood it, I coped better. The same was true of bodily changes to hair growth, the sound of a deepening voice and adjusting to greater sweatiness. Standing to pee helps me feel more male, but the fragrance of urine hitting my senses can be overwhelming. My good friend Emma advised me to drink more water (I don't recognize thirst), which helps dilute urine and stop the smell. Meeting other trans guys has also been totally enlightening and incredibly supportive. This is one of the reasons that role models are so important.

The physical, social, and emotional environment

The effects of an overly gendered social environment should also be considered. For example, having our environment soaked in a less gender-specific domain in educational settings can only benefit all. I know it can be argued that gendered environments help keep girls safe and many females don't want to be using a public toilet that male individuals have used. We need to keep 'private' and 'public' distinct in so many ways. So, although having toilets that are simply labelled 'toilet' is one way to fight transphobia, we need to consider the type of toilet on offer. The traditional male toilet that houses cubicles and stalls isn't conducive to being a transgender male who might not have the confidence to use a stall or have medically transitioned or feel safe in such an environment. Instead, we could have single, self-contained toilets (as opposed to those with shared sinks) and this might solve the concerns of both cis women and trans people about toilet safety:

> Despite all-gender toilets often being framed as only about trans people, all-gender toilets are beneficial for a range of people and situations: parents with children of a different gender; those who care for people of a different gender; some disabled people who have a personal assistant of a different gender; and some people whose gender is questioned in the toilet, including some trans and non-binary people (and, to a lesser extent, some cis people). The vast majority of women had no problem using 'all gender' toilets. (Slater & Jones, 2018)

Being open and willing to discuss these issues and not hide them is also important. At the same time, of course, doing so respectfully and being aware of personal privacy is of the utmost importance. Many places will have a washroom for males, one for females and one that is unisex.

I look forward to a world where acceptance of difference is

the norm. Are you less male because you choose to wear your hair long, or less female if you wear your hair short? If autism and gender are both spectrum dispositions, why the need to decide, concretely, on one or the other? As professionals, being prepared to journey with individuals says I respect you, trust you to arrive at the appropriate destination for this time, will support you along the way and will be here, beside you, as you tackle uncharted territories.

Safety

Creating a safe space for all of us, whatever our gender, and appreciating that gender is a spectrum that varies as much as autism does, needs to be understood and accommodated. Giving each person the right to find themselves and pursue their growing years with dignity and appropriate support sends all individuals the message they are valued – whatever their ability, gender disposition, personality, religion, race, sexuality or colour. Building the kind of future we can thrive in takes a commitment from each one of us.

Safety is a space and a place that looks different for each of us. For me, safety is represented by a lack of being judged, a commitment to justice, being heard and then having my story mean a sense of freedom to be myself. For others, safety may be represented within a family, an individual, a home that lets them shut the door. If we listen to others, we will hear what it is they need and if we cannot give it to them, we can find others who will.

Younger autistic people

Autism awareness and support is generally more available in western society. Of course, there are still waiting lists for assessment and identification. Not all schools work with a design which allows for individual differences. However, in an informed society, young autistic individuals often receive family support for the different ways they process information and for their differing learning styles (e.g. they may be encouraged to learn via technology, visuals, role play, music). Being given access to the right support when young is vital in improving outcomes in adulthood, and young autistic people need to be heard and believed when talking about their gender identity, as discussed in Chapter 3. Young autistic people grow up and become older autistic people. The way in which autism impacts older individuals differs in some ways from what is experienced in childhood. For example, older autistic people are more likely to make sense of facial and bodily expressions given out by others than autistic children (Lawson, 2015). This might be one reason younger autistic people may take a while to show gender discomforts or, quite the opposite, they may be very quick to notice these. I'm unsure why there is such a discrepancy across the spectrum, but I believe it to be a matter of connection.

Older autistic people

As one ages and faces daily encounters of failure over time, self-confidence may fall through the holes in the fabric of one's life, and the demands of life further outweigh the ability to cope. This may account, for example, for the reasons some research shows autistic adults fare poorly in the work force and their sense of well-being is lower than that of the general population (Geurts, Stek & Comijs, 2016). However, hyper-plasticity of the brain, often thought to be more prevalent in autistic people, may also contribute to either over-connectivity or under-connectivity with and between various brain regions, which impacts cognitive understanding. It is thought that plasticity declines less with time in autistic people (due to them starting out in life with more brain plasticity in the first place), than the non-autistic population (Oberman & Pascual-Leone, 2014). This could be an asset as it supports learning in ways where decline is more likely in the non-autistic population, (e.g. memory loss in the non-autistic population, compared to difficulties forgetting in the autistic population). It could again help explain why an autistic person who has not shown typical signs of gender dysphoria may suddenly announce they want to undergo gender transition when a switch is turned on and they connect the dots to numerous discomforts over time for the first time. I write about my own gender dysphoria and subsequent transition in my book *Transitioning Together* (Lawson & Lawson, 2017), in terms of joining the dots, as well as further expanding on my experiences as an autistic person who transitioned later in life in Chapter 12.

Conclusion

This chapter has sought to explain what being autistic and living with gender dysphoria might look like. I have tried to create wider understanding of why autism impacts gender incongruence, what helpful tools and ideas exist for addressing this and why it is important to listen to autistic people, suspend judgement and support our journey, at whatever place along the way we find ourselves. I hope this chapter helps to dispel some of the fears professionals might have in working with us. Neurodiversity includes everyone – autistic, neurotypical and everything in between. We all have sensory systems that connect us to inner and outer sensory information. One's sense of identity depends on being able to connect to the inner and outer map, or schema, of who we are, what we feel, what we think and where we feel at home. It's just that as autistic people we might be more disconnected from our sense of self, or we might know very well who we are, but not be socially skilled enough to know how to keep ourselves safe. I think about a young autistic trans woman I know who sees no problem wearing a bright, colourful frock walking down the high street in town. She is six foot tall, has a beard (too uncomfortable to shave) and a very deep voice and believes everyone should accept her just the way she is. Her viewpoint is right...but the reality she lives in currently does not reflect this, which may create various complications in her life. We are not yet at the place where our society is accepting and comfortable with difference and diversity. We are working on it, but, in the meantime, we need professionals who will accompany us on this journey, help explain things to us, set out the guidelines and support us until we know how to keep ourselves safe and truly be at home in our gender, even if it's not the one assigned to us at birth.

References

American Psychiatric Association (2013) *Diagnostic and Statistical Manual of Mental Disorders* (5th ed.). Arlington, VA: American Psychiatric Publishing.

Bakker, J. *et al.* (2018, May) 'Symposium. S30.3 Brain structure and function in gender dysphoria.' Presented at The European Society of Endocrinology Annual Meeting, Toronto.

Baron-Cohen, S. (1999) 'The Extreme Male-Brain Theory of Autism.' In H. Tager-Flusberg (ed.), *Neurodevelopmental Disorders*. Cambridge, MA: MIT Press.

Dattaro, L. (2020, September 14) 'Largest study to date confirms overlap between autism and gender diversity.' *Spectrum*. Available at www.spectrumnews.org/news/largest-study-to-date-confirms-overlap-between-autism-and-gender-diversity [accessed 27 April 2021].

Davies, S., McIntyre, S. & Rypma, C. (2019, April) *Detransition rates in a national UK gender identity clinic*. Third biennal EPATH Conference Inside Matters. On Law, Ethics and Religion, Rome, Italy. Available at https://epath.eu/wp-content/uploads/2019/04/Boof-of-abstracts-EPATH2019.pdf [accessed 27 April 2021].

Geurts, H.M., Stek, M. & Comijs, H. (2016) 'Autism characteristics in older adults with depressive disorders.' *American Journal of Geriatric Psychiatry*, 24, 161–169.

Goodall, E. (2016) *Interoception as a building block for wellbeing – both physical & mental health require self-connectedness* [Slides]. *Academia.Edu*. Available at www.academia.edu/30595958/Interoception_as_a_building_block_for_wellbeing_both_physical_and_mental_health_require_self_connectedness [accessed 27 April 2021].

Goodall, E. (2019) *Ready to learn: Interoception kit*. Government of South Australia, Department of Education. Available at www.education.sa.gov.au/doc/ready-learn-interoception-kit [accessed 23 February 2021].

Guerra, M.P., Balaguer, M.G., Porras, M.G., Murillo, F.H., Izquierdo, E.S. & Ariño, C.M. (2020) 'Transsexuality: Transitions, detransitions, and regrets in Spain.' *Endocrinología, Diabetes y Nutrición* (English ed.), 67(9), 562–567.

Heylens, G., Aspeslagh, L., Dierickx, J., Baetens, K. *et al.* (2018) 'The co-occurrence of gender dysphoria and autism spectrum disorder in adults: An analysis of cross-sectional and clinical chart data' *Journal of Autism Developmental Disorders*, 48(6), 2217–2223. doi:10.1007/s10803-018-3480-6.

Lai, M.C., Lombardo, M.V., Suckling, J., Ruigrok, A.N. V. *et al.* (2013) 'Biological sex affects the neurobiology of autism.' *Brain*, 136 (9), 2799–2815.

Lawson, W. (2011) *The Passionate Mind*. London: Jessica Kingsley Publishers.

Lawson, W. (2015) *Older Adults and Autism Spectrum Conditions: An Introduction and Guide*. London: Jessica Kingsley Publishers.

Lawson, W. & Dombroscki, B. (2017) 'Problems with object permanence: Rethinking traditional beliefs associated with poor theory of mind in autism.' *Journal of Intellectual Diagnosis and Treatment*, 5, 1–6.

Lawson, W. & Lawson, B. (2017) *Transitioning Together. One Couple's Journey of Gender and Identity Discovery*. London: Jessica Kingsley Publishers.

Leinung, M.C. & Jalaja, J. (2019) 'Changing demographics in transgender individuals seeking hormonal therapy: Are trans women more common than trans men?' *Transgender Health*, 5(4) 241–245. https://doi.org/10.1089/trgh.2019.0070.

Murphy, J., Prentice, F., Walsh, R., Catmure, C. & Bird, G. (2020) 'Autism and transgender identity: Implications for depression and anxiety.' *Research in Autism Spectrum Disorders*, 69, 1–11.

Murray, D., Lesser, M. & Lawson, W. (2005) 'Attention, monotropism and the diagnostic criteria for autism.' *Autism*, 9(2), 139–156.

Oberman, L.M. & Pascual-Leone, A. (2014) 'Hyperplasticity in autism spectrum disorder confers protection from Alzheimer's disease.' *Medical Hypotheses*, 83(3), 337–342.

Reardon, S. (2019) 'The largest study involving transgender people is providing long-sought insights about their health. The research examines once taboo questions about the impacts of gender transition.' *Nature*, 568, 446–449. https://doi.org/10.1038/d41586-019-01237-z.

Rudacille, D. (2016) 'Living between genders.' *Spectrum*. Available at www.spectrumnews.org/features/deep-dive/living-between-genders [accessed 27 April 2021].

Saleh, N. (2014, November 9) 'Link between autism and gender dysphoria?' *Psychology Today*. Available at www.psychologytoday.com/au/blog/the-red-light-district/201411/link-between-autism-and-gender-dysphoria [accessed 27 April 2021].

Sanbonmatsu, K. (2019) *The Biology of Gender, from DNA to the Brain* [Video]. Available at www.youtube.com/watch?v=HLEgiRiFsds [accessed 27 April 2021].

Slater, J. & Jones, C. (2018) 'Around the toilet: A research project report about what makes a safe and accessible toilet space.' Sheffield Hallam University.

van der Miesen, A.L.R., Hurley, H. & de Vries, A.D.C. (2016) 'Gender dysphoria and autism spectrum disorder: A narrative review.' *International Review of Psychiatry*, 28–1, 70–80. http://dx.doi.org/10.3109/09540261.2015.1111199.

Wiepjes, C.M., Nota, N.M., de Blok, C.J., Klaver, M. *et al.* (2018) 'The Amsterdam cohort of gender dysphoria study (1972–2015): Trends in prevalence, treatment, and regrets.' *The Journal of Sexual Medicine*, 15(4), 582–590.

Williams, A. (2017) 'Risk factors for suicide in the transgender community.' *European Psychiatry*, 41(S1), s894–s894.

Williams, S. (2018) 'Are the brains of transgender people different from those of cisgender people?' *The Scientist*. Available at www.the-scientist.com/features/are-the-brains-of-transgender-people-different-from-those-of-cisgender-people-30027 [accessed 23 February 2021].

Chapter 8

Developing a Good Relationship with an Autistic Transgender or Non-Binary Person as a Professional

Marianthi Kourti and Ella Griffin

Introduction

Working with transgender and non-binary autistic people as a professional requires attention to be paid to a variety of factors that may differ from your usual practice. Because support and services rarely adopt an intersectional approach in the way they are designed, as a professional you are likely to have more expertise providing support either to autistic people or to transgender and non-binary people (or possibly neither, depending on the focus of your profession). Working with someone who is both autistic and transgender/non-binary, therefore, will inevitably mean that you may have to reconsider some aspects of your practice and adjust these to their needs. In this chapter, we outline some aspects of professional support that may be specific to this group of people, and provide practical suggestions on how to deal with them. This is not tailored to a specific group of professionals, rather we are trying to address issues that occur in a variety of settings and services and challenge you to reflect on how these can be adapted in your own practice. We provide some examples from our own relationship, in the setting of specialist mentoring support, a type of support offered to autistic university students during their studies in the UK.

Marianthi is an autistic PhD researcher, specialist mentor for autistic university students and the editor of this book. They are also non-binary; however, they did not identify as such when they were supporting Ella, as their realization came after this relationship ended. They were very much at the learning stages of what it means to support and work with autistic transgender and non-binary people at the time, which may be useful for professionals who still have anxieties about 'getting it right' to know. They learned a lot from their relationships and sessions not only with Ella, but also with many other autistic transgender and non-binary students they supported over the years, and they are very grateful to all their students for their understanding and trust. Ella Griffin is a non-binary person who identifies with masculinity. They had Marianthi as an autism mentor for their foundation art course and are currently studying for a Master's in illustration. They discovered their identity though exploring their feelings around gender and presentation during sessions with Marianthi and beyond them.

Marianthi and Ella met when Ella was a first-year student, as Marianthi was assigned to be Ella's specialist mentor through their university studies. Although Marianthi's role was not to support Ella with gender identity issues in particular, as a specialist mentor they felt it was important with all students to discuss any mental health issues that may have a negative impact on their studies. With Ella in particular, discussing personal relationships, identity and sexuality became an important part of that. Ella did not identify as non-binary (at least during mentoring sessions) during the first year of university. They came out to Marianthi at the beginning of the second year, as part of a discussion around their anxiety and mental health problems. Marianthi and Ella then tried to develop a plan of support together about how to best address the discovery of their gender identity, along with the implications that it may have for their studies, social life and family relationships.

Forming a helpful mentality as a professional who works with trans and non-binary autistic people

Being a helpful professional towards transgender autistic and non-binary people starts before ever meeting the person you are supporting, by reflecting on your mentality and having an understanding of the issues that may arise in your work with the people you will be supporting. First, you must examine your own beliefs and biases around gender, gender identity, trans and non-binary people. More specifically, it might be worth asking yourself what your own beliefs are about what it means to be a man or a woman, why gender is a binary, what the connection is between gender and sex, how your profession in general and your role in particular deals with and perpetuates gender stereotypes, and how these stereotypes may affect both your own worldview and the type of support you are providing. There are some resources that can help you in this process. Gendered Intelligence,[1] a transgender-led charity that operates in the UK, provides free resources on its website regarding good practice when working with young trans and non-binary people (including those questioning and exploring gender identity). It can also provide training for places of education. Mermaids is a charity that has resources and support for younger transgender and non-binary people and those who work with them.

When it comes specifically to transgender and non-binary autistic people, you might want to consider your own views on the gendering of autism, as well as how being transgender and non-binary might be different for autistic people. Jessica Kingsley Publishers has recently published a couple of books about autistic transgender and non-binary people in particular alongside this one (Adams & Liang, 2020; Gratton, 2019). There are also many other resources referred to in other places in this book, as well as, of course, this book itself. It is hoped that much of what is written in this book, in this chapter and elsewhere, will be helpful to you in this process.

There are also a variety of areas that you might want to reflect on that are specific to your profession and your role in the lives of the

---

[1]   http://genderedintelligence.co.uk

people you support. Your reflections might be different depending on whether you primarily work with transgender and non-binary people or autistic people. Furthermore, your role might revolve specifically around support around people's gender identity, or this might be an issue that is peripheral to the type of support you are offering, as it was the case for us. Nevertheless, it is worth remembering that being trans and non-binary, particularly at the beginning of one's transition, can be all-consuming and affect all areas of life, as discussed in Chapter 7. So even if your support is not about that per se, it might be important for you to regularly check up on how the person you are supporting is dealing with it and consider various ways you might be able to support them in your own capacity.

An example of gendered practice that Marianthi reflected on is the gendered choice of university degrees. As a specialist mentor, they noticed that the choice of studies their students had made was often quite gendered, with men often studying science, technology, engineering and mathematic (STEM) subjects and women tending to study humanities and social sciences subjects. This is not uncommon in universities in the UK and across the world (Perez-Felkner, Nix & Thomas, 2017); however, after a while, Marianthi started wondering if it affected their expectations and approaches towards their students, whether they were cisgender, transgender and/or non-binary. For example, they noticed that they were developing different expectations of students' skills, based on how they were distributed across the fields, such as some students being able to produce written assignments better than others, which was consistent with overall stereotypes of gendered abilities in students (e.g. Blažev *et al.*, 2017; Guay *et al.*, 2010). This meant that there was a risk of an assumption of competence in some areas because of a student's gender, which could mean that, unknowingly, some areas in which the students struggled may have gone unnoticed because they, as a mentor, would forget to check on them. They also reflected on what that meant specifically for their transgender and non-binary students, their studies, and the attitudes of the departments they might study in, both among the university staff and among other students. Was it likely that some departments were more inclusive than others? And if so, which ones and what was the effect of this on the students? Marianthi's answer was not always to take a specific approach around this, but to make more of an internal commitment to regularly check their own attitudes and beliefs around this topic and make an active effort to notice any development of gendered stereotypes in their attitude towards all students.

Developing useful strategies

Another step that a professional can take towards forming the right attitudes regarding transgender and non-binary autistic people is to develop useful strategies and practices around the practical issues that might come up during their support. What you might need to work on will be different based on whether you primarily work with autistic people or transgender/non-binary people, given that you probably already have a variety of strategies to support the people with whom you are working. If you are primarily an autism professional, thinking about practical ways to tackle the pronouns of the people you support is really important, because respecting trans and non-binary people's pronouns is crucial for developing a good relationship with them, and there may also be coming-out-related safety concerns that you will need to discuss with them. Pronoun use is diverse and not equally important to all people, so it is best if this discussion is led by the person you are supporting. However, thinking about your overall approach to this issue in advance is likely to be beneficial to you.

Pronouns, as well as names, will be dealt with differently in verbal and written communication, so it is important to think about the kind of places and circumstances in which you might refer to someone by their name and pronouns. In verbal communication, think about how you are going to ask them about their pronouns. For example, in one-to-one support, the pronoun you are most likely to be using most of the time is 'you', since you will be talking directly to the person you are supporting. You are also unlikely to use the person's name to refer to them. Correct use of pronouns should also be independent of the person's presence in that space; in other words, it is not okay to misgender someone when they are not present, or in places they may not have access to. You can use spaces like your own personal notes or group meetings with other colleagues (where confidentiality allows) to practise using the correct pronouns for a person. Practising in written or spoken format ('they went to the shops' or 'that is xer pencil case') will make using the pronouns, particularly non she/he pronouns, easier, especially if you are unfamiliar with their use.

It is also important to think about how you are going to deal with mistakes around pronouns, which might be more likely to happen if, for example, you have been supporting someone for a while prior to their transition and are used to their old pronouns and name. When making a mistake in verbal communication, it is best to apologize quickly and move on, much like you would have done if you made a mistake about any other fact about that person, such as age or ethnicity. One of Marianthi's personal pet peeves as a non-binary person is pre-emptive apologies – professionals stating, often at the beginning of their support, that they will do their best to respect someone's pronouns, following it with a pre-emptive apology for when they get it wrong. Apologizing for something that has not been done yet implies that it will probably happen, so this statement, although probably not intended as such, comes across as if someone is saying that they will not try too hard to use the correct pronouns. It is also unfair to ask someone to 'forgive' you for something in advance, no matter how many times you get it wrong. It is like saying to someone, 'I will try not to hurt you, but if I do hurt you, I apologize.' It does not inspire confidence in you as a professional, and it does not help the person you are supporting to develop trust in you. It is also worth remembering that dealing with wrong names and pronouns is likely to be incredibly common in that person's life, so while you may only make that mistake a few times, they deal with it constantly and it can be exhausting. It is much better to say 'thank you for letting me know' when they share their name and pronouns with you, be mindful as much as you can, and if a mistake happens, apologize and move on. In one of our sessions, for example, Marianthi was telling Ella about something they were thinking about them when they were at home and used the wrong pronoun by mistake. Ella quickly corrected them, as Marianthi had not noticed that it had happened, and Marianthi apologized, moved on and treated the incident as a reminder to be more careful with pronouns in the future.

Mistakes in written communication – for example when you are contacting other people on behalf of the person you are supporting or writing reports about them and the type of support you are offering them – are often much harder to correct after the documents have been shared with others. Many trans and non-binary people find misgendering on documents more hurtful than verbal misgendering. After all, one can revisit a written communication repeatedly, while verbal communication is fleeting. It is, however, easier to correct a document by proofreading it for issues like that right after it is written, so take a few minutes to do so if you are concerned about making such a mistake. If the document is electronic, using 'find' and 'replace' can be a quick way to catch mistakes like that without making it time consuming.

Another issue you will need to consider regarding written communication and documents is who will have access to them, and whether they know that the person you are supporting is trans/non-binary. Make sure that you are aware who the person you are supporting has come out to, particularly at the early stages of their transition, as outing them may make them vulnerable to certain people and put them in danger as a result. Always keep in mind that you may know who will have access to the documents you are writing better than the person you are supporting, as they will probably not be aware of the structure of your workplace. Have an honest conversation with them about who may have access to these documents in order to give them the ability to choose who they are comfortable coming out to. This will probably not be a one-time conversation either; rather, you may have to check this regularly with them, depending on the kind of support you are providing to them.

If you are providing long-term support to an autistic transgender person or supporting someone in the latter stages of their transition, you might want to think about the extent to which a retroactive correction of records and documents about them is possible, and ask them if that is something they are interested in. It is worth remembering that even after a transgender person has finished transitioning, they are still at risk of being outed (and thus potentially being put in danger) if people and institutions have access to documents about them that state their old name and pronouns. It is also worth noting that, at least when it comes to official documents, how to deal with non-binary gender identities and pronouns can still be unclear, as they are not officially recognized. Think about how you and your workplace might deal with that tension and discuss it with the people you are supporting. However, be aware that this might be an upsetting topic for them. An additional risk for autistic people in this regard is that they may access a lot more services specifically because of their disability, which means a lot more records of them exist and it can be really daunting for them to track them all and get them changed. Furthermore, their executive function difficulties may get in the way, as also discussed in Chapter 5. Consider how you might be able to support them in this, including making them aware of all the different places that might keep records about them, since this may be something that they have not thought of, and it compromises their safety and their agency over their identity.

For professionals who work mainly with transgender and non-binary people, understanding how being autistic affects someone's understanding of their own gender identity can be crucial. Chapter 6 covers this topic further, from the perspective of someone working in a gender identity clinic. In addition to understanding how to support them to understand themselves, you may also need to be ready to discuss some of the practical implications of transitioning that may be more prevalent for autistic people, or that autistic people may not realize as quickly as non-autistic trans and non-binary people do, as is discussed in Chapter 7. Such examples might be relationships with family members, as autistic trans and non-binary people may be more dependent on their family members compared to their non-autistic peers, for reasons linked to their survival, even if their family is not accepting of their gender identity. Discussions over safety are, therefore, imperative; making sure that autistic transgender and non-binary people are aware of the risks they are taking by transitioning in a transphobic society is crucial for their safety and their emotional, physical and mental health. Also remember that being autistic does not invalidate a person's transness. Autistic people are often subject to infantilization, and our choices are consistently devalued specifically because of our autistic identity, which professionals in general, but arguably those who are not used to working with autistic people in particular, need to keep in mind.

Finally, it is worth remembering that if you are cisgender, there are certain things that you might be ignorant about, such as inter-community issues, certain gender identities and trans struggles. It is important, therefore, to be ready to listen to the person you are supporting, open about areas you might not know a lot about, and prepared to learn. Identities do not fit neatly into boxes and they change and evolve over time. Ella, for example, identifies as a non-binary male, yet still feels that label is just an approximation of their feelings about their gender. Marianthi realized their non-binary identity much later in life, and they view their gender as very fluid and contextual. Some individuals may just know they are not cisgender yet have no label. You might also need to be aware of the tensions in the community, particularly if your role brings people together in some way. For example, binary trans people sometimes hold prejudice against non-binary people, and this could cause conflict or friction if you want to create a support group or help people create friendships, although the majority of binary transgender people do not think this way. Furthermore, just because people are transgender or non-binary (or autistic!) does not mean that they will get along with each other. However, community support can be beneficial for many. It is always worth offering certain things, but be prepared to be led by the person you are supporting and their (possibly ever-changing) needs.

Forming a healthy and trusting relationship with the person you support

Forming a relationship that is healthy and trusting is essential for autistic transgender and non-binary people to be able to engage with you. In general, autistic, trans and non-binary people are often scared and sceptical in their interactions with professionals, specifically because of their past interactions with them. This is also why they are often very grateful to find a professional who is helpful and supportive. A relationship that is person-centred, validating, and safe will most certainly provide the best outcomes for the person you are supporting.

As stated above, Ella and Marianthi met a year prior to them realizing their non-binary identity. The first year working together focused on other issues that were affecting Ella, alongside university studies, such as friendships and romantic relationships. At the beginning of their second year, on returning from the summer break, during which they were not provided with specialist mentoring support (which is typical with mentoring), Ella's mental health was very poor. The first few sessions focused on unpicking what the underlying causes of their bad mental health were, and how these could possibly be addressed. After a couple of sessions, Ella said to Marianthi, 'You know, I think I am non-binary, I am not a girl' and Marianthi responded, 'Okay, thank you for letting me know. Feel free to talk about this as much or as little as you want.' It was never questioned, challenged or invalidated in any way; instead, Marianthi tried to be as encouraging as possible. If anything, Marianthi was relieved that Ella had identified the cause of their distress and there was now a practical goal that they could work towards and develop. Disclosing all of that and beginning the journey of self-realization was overwhelming for Ella and, had it not been addressed, it most definitely would have had a negative impact on their studies, which is what Marianthi was there to support them with.

After identifying how Ella felt about their gender identity, the sessions became a space where they could explore that a bit further and work out what the next steps they wanted to take might be. Marianthi tried to provide room for Ella to discover themself and their feelings and linked them up to local LGBTQ+ organizations that could provide further support outside mentoring. Together they worked on coming-out strategies and plans, and on how to deal with family, staff and students on their course and in other professional services, such as their doctor. They tried to manage the coming-out process in a way that was safe for Ella, both physically and emotionally. As

Ella had to engage with various professionals and services, which is something that they (as many autistic people tend to) struggled to do, Marianthi tried to help them navigate those communications and reach out to people on their behalf where possible. Marianthi also tried to prepare Ella as well as they could on how to deal with transphobic comments and reactions in a way that protected Ella's mental health, and tried to put them in touch with other autistic trans and non-binary people.

Not all this support was always helpful. Marianthi recalls one conversation where Ella was wondering how to make others not misgender them and how to make themself look more masculine, and Marianthi asked Ella whether they would consider cutting their hair short. Ella said that they liked their hair, and they did not want to cut it. In hindsight, this was perhaps not the best suggestion to make to begin with, as it put the burden of changing in the hands of someone who was vulnerable and was not the perpetrator of the unhelpful practice, and it might have raised expectations that others' reactions were going to change after the haircut was implemented, thus possibly setting them up for disappointment. However, because the relationship was good and Ella knew that Marianthi's suggestion, however unhelpful, was well intended, Ella moved on quickly from that. Ella did, however, later cut their hair short. Some suggestions may be the right ones, but not given at the right time in someone's life.

Transitioning steps, however big or small, can feel overwhelming. Autistic people have their own perceptions on transitioning that vary from one person to the other. For example, some people might not be interested in physically transitioning or be interested in only partial physical transition, something that should always be respected. As shown in the example above, even something as insignificant (in the sense that it is rectifiable, in time) as a haircut can feel like a big deal for some people, or can be an unwanted change. Furthermore, autistic people can have various sensory issues that hinder their transition; for example, chest binding or genital packing might be impossible because of sensory sensitivities. The growth of body hair for individuals taking testosterone may feel overwhelming, and sometimes relieving gender dysphoria may clash with the individual's sensory needs, which is even more of a reason to keep the support person-centred and empower the individual to make an informed decision. Further examples of these issues are presented in Chapter 7.

Examining and discussing the risks associated with various parts of physical and social transition is very important. For example, binding is a practice that carries a lot of risks, especially if done for prolonged periods of time, which is important for someone to know and then be able to evaluate their needs, sensitivities and other aspects of their life with someone safely, without feeling as if they may be swayed one way or the other. Ultimately, the goal of any support provided should be to improve mental health and alleviate any dysphoria felt, in whatever way this is done. The person you support might never settle on a name, pronoun or gender, or fit into any label or category, at least while they are supported by you. If, however, you have provided a safe space for them to explore who they are, to be able to discuss their thoughts and needs, and to feel supported in making their own decisions, some of the mental anguish that comes with being gender non-conforming and autistic will have been alleviated.

One final area that professionals will need to be mindful of when it comes to supporting autistic transgender and non-binary people is providing support during the transition out of the service. An aspect often overlooked by service providers, the transition out of a service or from one professional to another, is very important, especially if the person has developed a good relationship with someone and has come to depend on them and the service they provide. This is an issue that needs to be considered on an organizational level as well, as it cannot be the responsibility of a single professional. A variety of factors need to be considered, such as changes of circumstances for the professionals (parental leave, sick leave, contracts ending, etc.) as well as structural changes within the institution that may change the type of support or supporting person. One particular reason that this may be distressing for autistic transgender and non-binary people is because they will have to come out all over again to the new person supporting them, as well as renegotiating their boundaries and determining new rules of engagement. If possible, therefore, make sure that support for this transition is provided, and that it is also clear to the person which professionals know what. For example, let them know who they can talk to in case you are unavailable for a period of time, as well as what information that person knows about them. Discuss with them what they would like you to communicate to the rest of your colleagues and what they would rather disclose themselves. Keep in mind that just because they have shared a piece of information with you, it does not mean that they are happy for anybody else in your service to know, unless explicitly specified. The existence of both trans and non-binary people and autistic people often becomes the object of discussion and fascination for others in very uncomfortable ways, so it is worth noticing how that might be perpetuated through your service. Clear and user-led communication among staff members can also go a long way to alleviate undue stress and anxiety. One of Marianthi's regrets is that this support was not in place when they unexpectedly had to leave their role, and thus the students they supported, including Ella, lost their support abruptly and without a solid plan for how it would be continued.

Conclusion

In this chapter, we have outlined various aspects of forming a good relationship with an autistic transgender and non-binary person for the professional who supports them. Using our own relationship as mentor and mentee as an example, we have highlighted aspects of the support often provided to an autistic transgender and non-binary person so that you can consider your specific approaches, both on an individual and an organizational level. We have provided some examples of useful practice as it worked in our relationship as well as examples of what did not work, because we believe that this is equally important to highlight. Overall, we have tried to bring attention to some aspects of your support that might differ for this group of people from what you are used to providing, as autistic transgender and non-binary people as a group usually access services with professionals who specialize either in the autism or gender part of their identity and thus may not know how to engage with the part that is not their speciality. We also wanted to highlight how these two identities may intersect in a person to create sets of circumstances that are unique to them, and to make some suggestions for how to approach them. Of course, every professional relationship and type of support has its own role in a person's life as well as its own rules of engagement, so you will need to consider these in the context of your own work with the person you are supporting and adjust them accordingly. It is also worth noting that our own perceptions on and knowledge of what it means to be autistic and non-binary is always evolving and developing, so there may be more areas that we consider important in the future, or we may reconsider some of these suggestions. We do believe, however, that what we have provided in this chapter is a good starting point for any professional who wants to build a healthy, empowering and person-centred relationship with the transgender and non-binary people they support.

References

Adams, N. & Liang, B. (2020) *Trans and Autistic: Stories from Life at the Intersection.* London: Jessica Kingsley Publishers.

Blažev, M., Karabegović, M., Burušić, J. & Selimbegović, L. (2017) 'Predicting gender-STEM stereotyped beliefs among boys and girls from prior school achievement and interest in STEM school subjects.' *Social Psychology of Education,* 20(4), 831–847.

Gratton, F.V. (2019) *Supporting Transgender Autistic Youth and Adults: A Guide for Professionals and Families.* London: Jessica Kingsley Publishers.

Guay, F., Chanal, J., Ratelle, C.F., Marsh, H.W., Larose, S. & Boivin, M. (2010) 'Intrinsic, identified, and controlled types of motivation for school subjects in young elementary school children.' *British Journal of Educational Psychology,* 80(4), 711–735.

Perez-Felkner, L., Nix, S. & Thomas, K. (2017) 'Gendered pathways: How mathematics ability beliefs shape secondary and postsecondary course and degree field choices.' *Frontiers in Psychology,* 8, 386.

Part 3

LIVING at the Intersection of Autism and Trans and/or Non-Binary Experiences

Autism, Gender Variance and Alexithymia

OVERLAP, IMPLICATIONS AND RECOMMENDATIONS FOR PRACTICE

Alyssa Hillary-Zisk and Jo Minchin

Introduction

When we talk about sensory issues in autism, most people can understand that it is common for autistic people to have something different with their sight, hearing, taste, touch or smell. People who have been around us a bit longer are aware that there may be differences in our vestibular system, which basically tells us which way up we are, or our proprioception, which tells us where bits of us are in relation to other things. But very few people will talk about the sense of interoception, because very few people think about how they sense what is inside them. In this chapter, we discuss what interoception and alexithymia are, how they have been connected with the experiences of autistic people and how they may influence the experiences of autistic transgender and non-binary people, with some personal examples.

Interoception

Interoception can be broadly defined as our ability to perceive the state of our body. This includes things such as how hungry or thirsty we are, the feeling of our heart beating, an awareness of how fast we are breathing and so on (Craig, 2002). The degree of awareness of these processes can differ, and can incorporate both conscious and unconscious levels of information processing as well as both painful and non-painful stimuli (Barrett & Simmons, 2015). While a neurotypical person might have an intuitive awareness of their body's physical state, probing reveals that the concept of interoception is quite difficult to pin down. Interpretations of interoception vary somewhat in terms of which signals are considered to be interoceptive and how conscious the level of awareness of those signals (neuro) typically is. Some types of touch are considered interoceptive, whereas others are not (Khalsa & Lapidus, 2016).

It is also important to point out that interoception is not just one channel of information. Interoception is constant feedback from many different systems within the body. Most people with interoceptive signals within the relative field of 'normal' are most likely to be aware of the loudest signal at any given time (Critchley *et al.*, 2004). If someone is very hungry, that is most likely to be their overriding feeling, bothering them more than the slight headache they might have or the itch just below their knee. The definition of interoception is, therefore, a slightly contentious topic in neuroscience (Khalsa & Lapidus, 2016), but a good working definition refers to awareness of the state of one's own body. It might be helpful to think of interoception, and then the actions we take based on interoceptive signals, being a bit like the governor of an engine that keeps it ticking over at the right speed. Without it, the engine would overheat or break. At the very least, interoception encompasses awareness of any number of internal homeostatic feedback loops meant to maintain stable bodily functions.

Autistic people often have atypical interoception (Bird *et al.*, 2010). Then, one of the first things that an autistic person growing up in a neurotypical world learns, even if we do not know that we are autistic, is that the things we experience are not the same as those other people do. We often learn this by way of being told we cannot be experiencing what we are experiencing. This can be called 'social gaslighting'. Malice may or may not be involved. However, if several people are watching the same presentation and only one person thinks it is painfully loud, that one person may be taught to ignore (or at least keep quiet about) their perceptions. It is very hard to explain your feelings to others when you don't know if anyone else is experiencing them, or how they describe those feelings. This is frequently problematic for autistic people, as our interoceptive signals can diverge from the (statistical) norm and are often at odds with what everyone else reports. Is it not surprising, therefore, that this leads us to chronically overriding or tuning out these interoceptive signals, to the point that we do not trust anything that we are experiencing or feeling at all (Graigg, Cornell & Bird, 2018). It may be possible that some autistic people have naturally poor interoceptive signals, but others are forced to learn to repress them. (Both could also be occurring simultaneously, in the same person.) Transgender people may find this process relatable as well: bodily dysphoria is not shared by cisgender people of their assigned gender, and so our instincts can be explicitly denied.

Interestingly, there is overwhelming evidence for high rates of atypical interoception in many neurodivergent groups and/or groups with other mental health difficulties, including people diagnosed with feeding and eating disorders (Klabunde *et al.*, 2013), anxiety, and panic disorders (Pollatos & Schandry, 2008), alcohol and substance abuse (Paulus & Stewart, 2014), people with depression (Dunn *et al.*, 2007), somatoform disorders (Mussgay, Klinkenberg & Rüddel, 1999), obsessive compulsive disorder (Lazarov *et al.*, 2010), schizophrenia (Ardizzi *et al.*, 2016), post-traumatic stress disorder (PTSD) (Frewen *et al.*, 2008), and personality disorders (Mussgay *et al.*, 1999). So, rather than specifically an autism thing, atypical interoception could be a general neurodivergence thing, or it could be a distress thing.

In fact, Peter Vermeulen (2014), a Belgian scholar at Autisme Centraal, wrote about autism and happiness. Some 'autistic' traits such as being 'rigid' or 'fixed' are also (or actually) typical observations about stressed or uncomfortable people. And many autistic people deal with chronic stress or discomfort. Many autistic people also say their interoceptive signals are too strong and have to be drowned out. Regardless of why a person has difficulties with their interoceptive signals, alexithymia is a possible result.

Alexithymia

Alexithymia describes difficulty identifying and describing one's feelings, along with difficulty distinguishing them from physical states such as being hot, hungry or tired. Typically, these emotions and physical states are identified from interoceptive signals. About 5–8 per cent of people in general are alexithymic, but about 50 per cent of *autistic* people are (Hill & Berthoz, 2006; Hill, Berthoz & Frith, 2004). Both inherently divergent interoception or a need to consistently ignore sensory sensitivities and interoceptive signals could relate to alexithymia. At the same time, gender dysphoria can cause dissociation, again potentially leading to missed or ignored interoceptive signals, although this is an area that research has yet to explore. In short, we know the following:

- People with trauma histories are more likely to have alexithymia (Krystal, 1971; Zeitlin, McNally & Cassiday, 1993).

- Several other neurotypes or conditions, often also associated with autism, come with increased rates of alexithymia.

- Autistic people have higher rates of trauma and PTSD than the general population, including from events the *Diagnostic and Statistical Manual of Mental Disorders* (American Psychiatric Publishing, 2013) may not consider traumatic (Rumball, Happé & Grey, 2020).

- LGBTQ people, including transgender people, *also* have increased rates of traumatic events and PTSD compared to the general population (Wawrzyniak & Sabbag, 2018).

- About half of autistic people have alexithymia, which is about ten times the rate in the general population (Kinnaird, Stewart & Tchanturia, 2019).

- Alexithymia is likely related to difficulties with interoception or sensing and identifying what is *physically* happening in our bodies (Brewer, Cook & Bird, 2016; Murphy, Catmur & Bird, 2018).

While research considering autism, alexithymia and transgender identity together is, to our knowledge, yet to be produced, these facts suggest that anyone working with transgender autistic people is reasonably likely to be working with transgender autistic people who *also* have alexithymia and its associated interoception issues. Therefore, it makes sense to understand the combination as best we can. Specific research is needed, but only if it works from the basic assumption that transgender, autistic, alexithymic people really are all three, whether or not there are any causal relationships among them. That is, while all three are complicated enough that no one is likely to directly cause any of the others, causation *cannot* be relevant to the validity of autistic or transgender identity. (It may be relevant to trying to reduce alexithymia if someone would like to try.)

What is it like to be autistic, transgender and alexithymic? Some of Alyssa's experiences

Given the rate of alexithymia in autistic people, we might expect about half of the descriptions of the transgender autistic experience to in fact be descriptions of all three experiences. Given associations between trauma and alexithymia, as well as between transgender identity and trauma, it might even be more than half. In any case, other discussions of transgender autistic experience are relevant. Finn Gratton's (2019) discussion of transgender autistic experience in *Supporting Transgender Autistic Youth and Adults: A Guide for Professionals and Families* covers experiences that would be common for alexithymic and autistic trans people. However, Gratton does not specifically discuss alexithymia, and there does not seem to be much (if anything) written specifically about the overlap of all three experiences. Since I am non-binary, autistic and alexithymic, I can shed some light on this combination.

First, difficulty identifying and describing emotions is extremely different from a *lack* of emotions. Instead, it means that I may feel something is wrong without a full understanding of why, or that I may need to identify my emotional state based on cues other than the direct internal sense of emotions I am assuming some people have.

Rather than immediately knowing I am frustrated, I will notice that something is not working, that I am even more physically tense than usual, and possibly that my voice has got louder, that I am shaking, and/or that I am crying or on the edge of crying. From this evidence, I conclude that I am, in fact, frustrated.

For transgender people with alexithymia, this means we feel our gender dysphoria, and we may even act on it, but that does not mean we can identify or explain what it is we are feeling. Why we feel that way is even harder to explain.

In terms of social dysphoria, I knew from a very young age that I did not belong in 'girls' and 'women's spaces and activities, but I was a graduate student by the time I could explain *why*. According to my mother, I quit ballet when I was about three, not because I disliked it, but because it was an all-girls' class. I was not yet able to explain that I was not a girl, but I knew I did not belong in that class.

This non-belonging in women's spaces has continued to manifest. While I enjoyed singing and generally sought to join more singing groups in high school, my longest-lived attempt at joining treble choir, the girls' ensemble, lasted about a month, and it was deeply uncomfortable for many reasons. My being a tenor and not an alto did not help, but it was neither the entirety of the problem nor my primary issue.

My college involvement in the Society for Women Engineers was similarly short lived, and for much the same reasons: even before I could articulate that I am not, in fact, a woman, I still felt the emotional disconnect between who I am and who the space was for.

Instead, I felt more comfortable in mixed spaces, including spaces where I was the only non-man. Therefore, my friends from middle school and high school were primarily boys. Lunch tables were somewhat fluid and were not completely divided by gender, but I was the only non-boy at my usual table in middle school. If the rest of a group was going to be the same gender, and I was going to be the only person of a different gender present, I was much more comfortable if everyone knew that to be the case. After my failed attempt at joining treble choir, I was perfectly comfortable joining tenor bass choir, which was theoretically only open to male members of the main school chorus.

As another example, I hated being made to wear dresses, but once the event for which I had been made to wear the dress was over, I did not necessarily want to take the dress off. As an autistic and alexithymic child, I was not yet able to explain why this was. I still have the same discomfort with the expectation of skirts. I am also still perfectly comfortable with skirts themselves, when the expectation that I wear them is absent. Now, however, I can explain the distinction. A dress or a skirt is a piece of fabric. Many people attach a gender to it, but it is not inherently gendered. The dress or skirt will not induce gender dysphoria for me.

However, dress codes that specify skirts or dresses for certain events are gendered. There is no physical item to which people are collectively adding a gender for a good reason: it is a rule that is only ever about gender. People incorrectly assumed that I was a girl and applied a 'girl' rule to my behaviour and presentation. This is where I had a problem, and the problem was dysphoria.

I had the chance to address my discomfort with gender-specific dress codes in my final two years of high school, while I was in tenor bass choir. Typically, women wore a uniform blouse and skirt, while men wore a uniform tux shirt and vest with their own black dress trousers. Because tenor bass choir was the 'men's choir, but I was not a man, there was a legitimate question of whether I should wear the men's uniform to match my group or the women's uniform to match the gender people assumed me to have. In a truly impressive display of acting on my feelings while failing to identify them, the day before a concert, I asked, 'For the purpose of this ensemble, what will my gender be at 7.30pm tomorrow?'

No, I had not yet realized I was non-binary. Yes, I wore the men's uniform for the concert in question.

My physical dysphoria followed a similar pattern to my social dysphoria: I knew there was a problem, but it took years to understand *why* it was a problem. When puberty arrived, so did breasts. This was *unacceptable*. I started trying to bind my chest *immediately*, shortly before my eleventh birthday (I used too-small sports bras for most of this time, and I acquired commercial binders in my mid-twenties). I did not understand *why* I had this problem with my chest, or why binding was necessary, until my early twenties.

This delay meant an even longer delay in getting gender-affirming surgery in the form of a bilateral double mastectomy with masculine reconstruction. My surgery happened in between agreeing to write this chapter and sitting down to write it, nearly 17 years after the start of puberty when I recognized that my breasts were not, in fact, supposed to be there.

After surgery, I am still alexithymic. I am still autistic. Social dysphoria remains an issue at times. I typically ask to put my pronouns in my contact details for academic publications. The Institute of Electrical and Electronics Engineers (IEEE) Transactions on Neural Systems and Rehabilitation Engineering now has 'Mx' as a salutation option because they added it when I asked for it (after my leaving the salutation box blank led to an incorrect one – ouch!). *Physical* dysphoria, however, is no longer an issue. I pay both less and more attention to my body.

I pay less attention to my body in the sense that I am less focused on the *wrongness* on my chest. Physical dysphoria was distracting, and it was attention to my body. It was a persistent signal that something was *wrong*, and it is gone. It is not taking up bandwidth anymore, and that bandwidth is now free for other internal signals.

That ties into how I pay more attention to my body. I do not think my interoception has improved, per se. However, with the bandwidth previously occupied by physical dysphoria now free for other signals, I have a better chance of noticing them. I also dissociate less. I have known for years, intellectually, that my shoulders are probably uneven due to my scoliosis. I could never look at myself well enough to tell you which shoulder was lower until after my surgery and the resulting resolution of my physical dysphoria. (My right shoulder is lower.) Since surgery, I have also noticed that my ribs are somewhat flared. I do not know if that could be related to nearly 17 years of binding, starting shortly before my eleventh birthday – most people *strongly* arguing that children that age should not bind seem to have other anti-trans opinions, and I do not think anyone has researched it properly. I also don't especially care. I can breathe fine and making it *to* surgery was more important than whether or not anyone would hire me as a chest model after surgery.

What should you keep in mind when working with people who might be autistic, transgender and alexithymic?

- We may know something is a problem (e.g. my breasts were 'not supposed to be there') but not be able to explain *why*, especially to people who expect feelings to be part of a 'proper' explanation.

- Dysphoria can cause an increase in dissociative experiences, which can make alexithymia and interoception issues *worse*. That is, the exact same dysphoria that we need to address is forcing us to be less in touch with our feelings and physical states just to cope.

- Be very aware of any history of (or ongoing) therapy goals or other professional interactions that may have pushed us to ignore internal signals, whether physical or emotional. Most directly, this means therapy goals directly about behaviour in line with a person's assigned gender at birth, despite the possibility that the person is transgender. This definitely happens (de Vries *et al.*, 2010), though we are not certain how common it is. However, this also includes any compliance-based therapy such as applied behaviour analysis, regardless of the goals. It also includes attempts at desensitization for sensory processing issues, as well as for things we may have avoided for gender reasons that were misinterpreted as being for sensory or other reasons. If we are explicitly taught to ignore the internal signals that could be translated into feelings (if with difficulty), this will, again, make it harder to describe our feelings. Do not punish us for the ways we have already been punished.

References

American Psychiatric Publishing (2013) *Diagnostic and Statistical Manual of Mental Disorders* (5th ed.). Arlington, VA: American Psychiatric Publishing.

Ardizzi, M., Ambrosecchia, M., Buratta, L., Ferri, F. *et al.* (2016) 'Interoception and positive symptoms in schizophrenia.' *Frontiers in Human Neuroscience*, 10, 379.

Barrett, L.F. & Simmons, W.K. (2015) 'Interoceptive predictions in the brain.' *Nature Reviews Neuroscience*, 16(7), 419–429.

Bird, G., Silani, G., Brindley, R., White, S., Frith, U. & Singer, T. (2010) 'Empathic brain responses in insula are modulated by levels of alexithymia but not autism.' *Brain*, 133(5), 1515–1525.

Brewer, R., Cook, R. & Bird, G. (2016) 'Alexithymia: a general deficit of interoception.' *Royal Society Open Science*, 3(10), 150664.

Craig, A. (2002) 'How do you feel? Interoception: The sense of the physiological condition of the body.' *Nature Reviews Neuroscience*, 3, 655–666.

Critchley, H.D., Wiens, S., Rotshtein, P., Öhman, A. & Dolan, R.J. (2004) 'Neural systems supporting interoceptive awareness.' *Nature Neuroscience*, 7(2), 189–195.

de Vries, A.L., Noens, I.L., Cohen-Kettenis, P.T., van Berckelaer-Onnes, I.A. & Doreleijers, T.A. (2010) 'Autism spectrum disorders in gender dysphoric children and adolescents.' *Journal of Autism and Developmental Disorders*, 40(8), 930–936.

Dunn, B.D., Dalgleish, T., Ogilvie, A.D. & Lawrence, A.D. (2007) 'Heartbeat perception in depression.' *Behaviour Research and Therapy*, 45(8), 1921–1930.

Frewen, P.A., Dozois, D.J., Neufeld, R.W. & Lanius, R.A. (2008) 'Meta-analysis of alexithymia in posttraumatic stress disorder.' *Journal of Traumatic Stress: Official Publication of the International Society for Traumatic Stress Studies*, 21(2), 243–246.

Graigg, S.B., Cornell, A.S. & Bird, G. (2018) 'The psychophysiological mechanisms of alexithymia in autism spectrum disorder.' *Autism*, 22(2), 227–231. (First published in 2016.)

Gratton, F.V. (2019) *Supporting Transgender Autistic Youth and Adults: A Guide for Professionals and Families*. London: Jessica Kingsley Publishers.

Hill, E.L. & Berthoz, S. (2006) 'Response to "Letter to the editor: The overlap between alexithymia and Asperger's syndrome", Fitzgerald and Bellgrove, *Journal of Autism and Developmental Disorders*, 36 (4).' *Journal of Autism and Developmental Disorders*, 36(8), 1143–1145.

Hill, E., Berthoz, S. & Frith, U. (2004) 'Brief report: Cognitive processing of own emotions in individuals with autistic spectrum disorder and in their relatives.' *Journal of Autism and Developmental Disorders*, 34(2), 229–235.

Khalsa, S.S. & Lapidus, R.C. (2016) 'Can interoception improve the pragmatic search for biomarkers in psychiatry?' *Frontiers in Psychiatry*, 7, 121.

Kinnaird, E., Stewart, C. & Tchanturia, K. (2019) 'Investigating alexithymia in autism: A systematic review and meta-analysis.' *European Psychiatry*, 55, 80–89.

Klabunde, M., Acheson, D.T., Boutelle, K.N., Matthews, S.C. & Kaye, W.H. (2013) 'Interoceptive sensitivity deficits in women recovered from bulimia nervosa.' *Eating Behaviors*, 14(4), 488–492.

Krystal, H. (1971) 'Trauma: Consideration of Severity and Chronicity.' In H. Krystal & W. Niederland (eds), *Psychic Traumatization*. Boston, MA: Little Brown.

Lazarov, A., Dar, R., Oded, Y. & Liberman, N. (2010) 'Are obsessive–compulsive tendencies related to reliance on external proxies for internal states? Evidence from biofeedback-aided relaxation studies.' *Behaviour Research and Therapy*, 48(6), 516–523.

Murphy, J., Catmur, C. & Bird, G. (2018) 'Alexithymia is associated with a multidomain, multidimensional failure of interoception: Evidence from novel tests.' *Journal of Experimental Psychology: General*, 147(3), 398.

Mussgay, L., Klinkenberg, N. & Rüddel, H. (1999) 'Heartbeat perception in patients with depressive, somatoform, and personality disorders.' *Journal of Psychophysiology*, 13(1), 27–36.

Paulus, M.P. & Stewart, J.L. (2014) 'Interoception and drug addiction.' *Neuropharmacology*, 76(B), 342–350.

Pollatos, O. & Schandry, R. (2008) 'Emotional processing and emotional memory are modulated by interoceptive awareness.' *Cognition & Emotion*, 22(2), 272–287.

Rumball, F., Happé, F. & Grey, N. (2020) 'Experience of trauma and PTSD symptoms in autistic adults: Risk of PTSD development following DSM-5 and non-DSM-5 traumatic life events.' *Autism Research*, 13(12), 2122–2132.

Vermeulen, P. (2014) 'The Practice of Promoting Happiness in Autism.' In G. Jones & E. Hurley (eds), *Good Autism Practice: Autism, Happiness and Wellbeing*. Birmingham: BILD Publications.

Wawrzyniak, A.J. & Sabbag, S. (2018) 'PTSD in the Lesbian, Gay, Bisexual, and Transgender (LGBT) Population.' In C.B. Nemeroff & C. Marmar (eds), *Post-Traumatic Stress Disorder*. Oxford: Oxford University Press.

Zeitlin, S.B., McNally, R.J. & Cassiday, K.L. (1993) 'Alexithymia in victims of sexual assault: An effect of repeated traumatization?' *The American Journal of Psychiatry*, 150(4), 661–663.

Chapter 10

The Resonant Self

MASKING, SCRIPTING AND PRECOGNITION IN AUTISTIC TRANSGENDER AND NON-BINARY PEOPLE

Lexi Orchard

Introduction

This chapter dives into the terminology and techniques of 'passing', something that is a way of life found throughout marginalized minorities, with extensive works on the topic in the areas of race, sexuality and gender. It consists of the culmination of decades of experience which is being explored and deconstructed to give insight into the world of passing from a singular unique vantage point. Building on that wisdom and experience there is an in-depth exploration of the impact and emotional cost of these approaches to remaining safe at work, at home and in social situations. Leading on from that, this chapter also covers the loss of that privilege and safety, and the consequences of being openly redefined by society. Written with the hope of shining a light on this topic, which rarely gets the time it deserves in academic or professional worlds, this chapter seeks to provide an instructive and supportive aid to those who have never considered the world of a passing autistic, non-binary person, or a person of any intersection of identities. Whether you are a professional looking to gain insight or a person trying to find someone 'like me', there is something for everyone in this introspection on passing as a non-binary autistic person.

When reading this chapter, please keep in mind that I struggle with terminology, with labels applied to people and the way we are all defined externally – forever being placed within boxes that fit others' definition of us. If you look for me on a chart in a presentation, you'll probably find me in the 'trans' section of that chart in autism studies, or the 'other' section of trans studies. It is unlikely that you would find a multitude of works on the non-binary, trans and autistic intersectionality, but that is thankfully beginning to change. Intersectionality is still a very new concept in the dynamics of a scientific study and is not applied nearly as much as perhaps it should be, particularly outside academia and activism.

The terminology of passing

Passing is a global term for a series of behaviours and processes employed by countless minorities or sub-cultures to protect themselves from harm and discrimination in society. The processes of masking (or camouflage), scripting and precognition are tools in an arsenal of passing found in race, sexuality, gender and autism settings, to name but a few. The process of passing is not absolute, has no complete form and can be a composite of many aspects of the areas I will explore in this chapter. There is often no validation of failure or success at the process of passing and in many ways the true goal of passing is to blend into the background of the world. Most imagine themselves the hero of their own story; I at best hope to be an extra in the story of my own life, unseen and safe from harm.

Another important term that I often use to explain my thought process and experiences is precognition. Precognition refers to the act of processing possible outcomes of a social interaction prior to it happening and scripting a reaction to each one of those in advance. As Ani Seth, a cognitive neuroscientist, once said, 'We predict ourselves into existence', which in reference to the social concept of 'self' defines precognition perfectly. To understand precognition, you need to visualize every interaction you have ever had, whether buying a bottle of milk from the local shop or talking to a neighbour.

Imagine the start of the interaction as a trunk of a metaphorical tree, with each action and reaction a branch on that tree, such as a manly handshake or firm eye contact. Continue that metaphor with every possible outcome being the leaves of the tree. This tree, or roadmap, of successful and failed outcomes based on the situation and circumstance of the engagement, would be considered as mapping 'win states', with a strong incentive to steer interaction away from negative outcomes and avoid harm.

Masking is the act of supressing your sense of identity until it no longer exists; to burn away every facet of your being, to erase from the world any image of yourself that society deems unacceptable in order to go unnoticed in daily life. To an autistic person, this might mean suppressing stimming in public. Gender non-conforming individuals are compelled to dress as society expects: feminine pinks for girls, expressions of visual masculinity for men, in line with their predominant cultural norms. To choose to put on cowboy boots rather than wearing my six-inch heels or to stop myself tapping the table rhythmically when desperate to stim are acts not brought about by shame, but external pressure to remain safe from harm – to exist hidden to the world, unheard, unseen, unknown in every moment of my daily routine. Masking (or camouflaging) is also discussed in Chapters 2 and 4 of this book.

Scripting is the performative act of outward expression that often seems to be conflated with masking or omitted when people talk about it. Scripting is the process of acting on a stage to an audience or presenting a form or character other than myself; a process to consciously mimic those seen around me, adopting peers' behaviours, behaviours seen in television, movies, or online mediums such as YouTube and other social media platforms. This can also involve constructing a series of personas, collating socially acceptable sources of outward behaviour into a composite to be used to survive future social interactions where precognition is not possible. Adopting others' behaviours in the moment or building a composite persona is a defence mechanism to blend into society and replace those behaviours of your identity being masked intentionally.

The impact and emotional cost of masking, scripting and precognition

When people look at me, their first instinct is to say, 'You don't look autistic.' If you comprehend the idea of gender beyond heteronormative labels of sex, you would have never thought 'non-binary' when seeing me. A decade ago, I wasn't diagnosed as autistic nor aware of what gender meant beyond what the 90's action movies had failed to teach me. You'd have seen a white, extroverted, perfectionist, cisgender man in a male-dominated sector of a well-paid industry. Every aspect of what you saw was engineered, refined, rehearsed and controlled down to the lowest level of minutiae. For 30 years, I managed to pass in plain sight, hidden from the prejudices of the world I blended into, too afraid to express myself since I was six years old. Prior to diagnosis, I was stalked by many labels, such as 'creative', 'intelligent', 'talented', 'eccentric', 'contrary', witty' and more. Soon those labels changed to 'different', 'weird', 'savant', 'rude', even 'low functioning' on a bad day. Within months of my diagnosis, I was exiled from work, friendships and a life I'd built passing, masking and scripting my way through every moment since beginning school.

My diagnosis as autistic and my realization of being non-binary have not, in either case, been the epiphany I have seen talked about by others online. Nor was there a liberation of expression that helped me 'find myself'. Quite the opposite: I am now 'other', at an intersection of gender and neurodiversity that a Venn diagram would signal as unemployment, stigma, rejection and fear from those around me. Those labels of my youth have been torn away and replaced by 'dangerous', 'unstable', 'unable', 'disabled', 'mentally ill', 'damaged'. I hate labels, even more now than I did when they were heralded at me as positives. I couldn't relate to them, or felt uneasy as others defined me or rather defined the masks I wore or the personas I put out into the world. That is not because of their meaning but because I felt so divorced from any of them. I felt trapped in this cycle of performance, unable to express or even fathom my own sense of identity in a quest to facilitate what others wanted me to be.

Using the techniques of passing, scripting and precognition often comes at a high level of personal cost for the individual that is using them. Having spent over three decades passing to be what others needed me to be, it is difficult to write this chapter without feeling a sense of regret, of loss. I am often left with a sense of wonder of who I would be today if I had not felt the need to pass for most of my life. For many of the years that I outwardly presented as a cisgender man I would hear words such as 'talented', 'intelligent', 'eccentric', 'extroverted', even 'considerate' or 'thoughtful' at times, used to describe me. The reality was the stark opposite: confused about my gender, feeling different and plagued by a sense of being unsafe to express who I was around anyone at school, home, work or in social settings. I felt drained and overwhelmed constantly, preparing the 'right' thing to say or do for every situation and repressing my feelings and thoughts to the point I lost sight of who 'I' was a lot of the time. This was something I personally was ill-equipped to express to anyone or verbalize even in safe spaces, an experience also discussed in Chapter 9.

The need to pass is ever-present, and it is often hard to describe just how much the risk of failure looms in every interaction I had on a daily basis. When I was diagnosed with autism at the age of 32, I told *one* person about my diagnosis and within hours a flood of hurtful messages from friends and work colleagues appeared. Headhunters who had begged for me to come work for them suddenly told me I'd be lucky for find contract work let alone a full-time position given my diagnosis. This humiliating and isolating experience of rejection will often be replicated for others more than once, especially considering the intersectionality of gender and autism diagnoses that can happen at different times in life. Countless times I saw those who did not mask their gender non-conformity or neurodiversity and how they were rejected in interviews on the basis of prejudice and confusion behind closed doors after they had left the situation. This only reinforced my own continued sense that passing was essential to survive in so many environments. As a result, passing seemed to me like the better option when compared with harm or discrimination.

It is not only social or work environments that are dangerous for so many people of marginalized identities to be open in. Many institutions in society are often inaccessible when we express ourselves openly. The social environments of these institutions force people to intentionally withhold information about themselves and to behave 'as expected'. The report by the Scottish Trans Equality Network (Valentine, 2016, p.27) entitled 'Non-binary people's experiences in the UK' highlighted that non-binary individuals felt that many services made them uncomfortable about disclosing their identities: 'The service where people felt the least comfortable being open about being non-binary was with the police, with 69% of respondents saying they "never" felt comfortable sharing their identity.' I am terrified of police officers and have experienced violence and physical assault on several occasions for no more than 'looking suspicious'. The National Health Service (NHS) is another example where being non-binary becomes problematic, with the same report highlighting that '50% of respondents said they "never" felt comfortable' with disclosing their gender to a doctor – and that is without considering the intersection of autism. This immediately diminishes the ability of the doctor to empathize, prevents referral to services such as an NHS gender identity clinic, and creates barriers in a relationship that should be built on trust. Furthermore, the gender-reassignment process in England is essentially only interested in sexual reassignment and has little to no understanding of a non-binary identity. Considering the high levels of unemployment in autistic populations, this will almost certainly disqualify a transgender autistic person from gaining gender certification in the UK because 'you are not living your gender in the world', which is one of the criteria of the process. Furthermore, a non-binary autistic person is unable to undergo the gender-certification process granting them access to medication and surgery in England. I am five years at least from even an initial consultation with a gender clinic, with waiting times growing exponentially.

Unfortunately, there are no easy answers on how to deal with these issues, nor little way of a compromise whether and when to 'pass'. For example, precognition, masking and scripting can be very detrimental to the success of a process such as counselling, therapy or other support services for mental health, often making it even more difficult to reach out for help when we are struggling. The resources available are far from helpful; often someone trying to find a therapist or group may have to travel hundreds of miles to find someone trained or willing to take them on, and spend hundreds of pounds per session without any certainty of the outcome. In my experience, the cognitive behavioural therapy (CBT) models provide a ruleset to facilitate a measure of progress and will give an autistic person such as myself a clear path to 'win' (getting the defined outcome of success), without actually gaining anything meaningful from it. I myself have done the same and found little improvement in my well-being but 'won' the CBT and given the practitioner a pay cheque in the process.

There is also a real concern for vulnerable individuals when services such as counselling are not aware of the complexities and are rife with failings of an outdated and harmful industry. For someone who is non-binary or autistic, the difficulties of finding a counsellor can be extremely troubling. With the practice of autistic and transgender conversion therapy commonplace, and the use of restrictive models of therapy which often exclude autistic people let alone further distinctions of their diversity or identity, it is evident that issues surrounding the comprehension of intersectional experiences are widespread and emblematic throughout the industry. Even with non-faith-based accreditation, it is important to examine their models, beliefs and practices before engaging in their care. Unfortunately, receiving support from therapy or NHS mental health services comes with a risk of these contributing to negative reinforcement and possibly even generating disorders such as PTSD. Many of these service providers have no autism or gender training, and a handful at best have both. A provider with a progressive view of one aspect of our identities may have a set of archaic views of the other aspects, as most work in an isolated and specialist field with no consideration for intersectionality. There is a sickening irony that the most vulnerable and isolated require such depth of effort to safeguard themselves from harm in an industry there to help them.

Precognition is a powerful tool to foresee the dangers ahead of us every day and helps prepare people with intersectional identities to pass in upcoming situations, removing as much real-time effort in the interactions we have day to day. However, it comes with the high cost of the physical effort and mental energy expended and the consequences that accompany that. To me, Pierre-Simon Laplace's reference to causal determinism, often termed 'Laplace's Demon' (Kožnjak, 2015), is a fairly accurate analogy for precognition, asserting that if an intelligence could commit to memory the present state of the universe, the future and past would be 'present before their eyes'. Consider this as one extreme of the process for a moment and a more sedate example such as someone preparing for what they say at an interview as the opposite 'end' of a spectrum of 'prediction'. The line or gradient of 'prediction' and when to apply it can become overwhelming, obsessive and often take over a person's life, causing them to lose touch with reality while constantly predicting the future. My own experience of this process has been a constant mindset for over 30 years and has become subconscious to the point of severe disassociation, visualizing interactions I know will come up and attempting to discern possible futures and how they will play out. Even in real-time I have attempted to use precognition at great cost to my social and mental strength, and at the risk of burnout.

By far the most negative cost of precognition I found for myself is existing in a permanently virtual state of potential futures, unable to process, enjoy or cherish what is happening in the moment. Reality itself can become indistinguishable from the various possible outcomes. Jumping from one interactive 'tree' to the next over the course of several chained interactions and desensitized from being emotionally engaged in the moment over attempting to 'win' the situation can become intoxicating. The downside of this is that I struggle with abrupt changes to preconceived events that will occur. I might start to meltdown if a meeting is moved forward a day, or the participants change suddenly, or someone is late. It is also vital to understand not only the social conventions of an interaction but also the rules by which to determine 'success' or 'failure' states. These vary wildly from person to person, situation to situation, based on their own cumulative experiences and those that made the most impact whether positive or negative. It is unlikely two people using this system of precognition will foresee exactly the same outcomes every time, and it is highly personal in nature.

Using these techniques for many years has had a profound and lasting impact that has dramatically affected my mindset in social situations. For example, I will openly become cynical when confronted with praise or positive validation of myself, whether presenting a talk or garnering compliments on my appearance. The idea someone can find me attractive or talented in any way makes me immediately suspicious of their motives and I begin to question their reasons for sentiments that I find difficult to believe. This has made building social connections extremely difficult. I also find it very hard to trust or take things at face value, overthinking and evaluating every minor action as a piece of a puzzle. Something that was very difficult for me to reconcile was the transitory nature of social relationships, family connections and the environments I found myself in and how they may not be the repetition of negative experiences from the past. This understanding is extremely difficult to process, but vital to allow the person you are to grow and your identity to evolve, to change. The person we presented as in high school or around our parents may no be longer necessary as a persona when entering university. As we grow older, move cities, and change jobs, we are given countless opportunities to adjust dramatically how we behave and interpret what the world we exist in wants from us. Something that was necessary in our childhood may be long since lost to our evolving lives and can be let go of. Personas will become outdated with time and circumstances, requiring huge amounts of social reintegration, with those around you only adding pressure on you to maintain the 'relevant' personas'.

Change can be a terrifying process on its own, especially when intertwined with disorders such as PTSD that continually reaffirm the need to remain safe from the ghosts of our past. Anyone given the chance to be free of those painful trappings of the past should get the most support possible to be themselves, or more importantly who they want to be in the moment. To this day, I still consider myself a reflection of the negative feedback I received early in life. I will often internalize a single event over and over in my mind, especially when the outcome of an event reinforces this negative image of myself. This is a consequence of scripting and masking for so long and creates negative barriers to change or self-acceptance. We may despise the personas we've built to survive, fully aware of the fundamental betrayal of who we are, but so often they feel necessary to keep us safe. Others will have received so much negative feedback that the person they want to be is internally rejected as unfit for their social ecosystem, as is my experience. This can lead to immeasurable levels of bitterness and self-loathing over time, as well as a tunnel vision that avoids new experiences and social engagements.

The painful cost of surviving

Even with the best of intentions and a deep empathy towards the person you are working with, helping someone accept who they want to be and work towards diminishing passing is not without consequences. After decades of focusing on the external demands of others, I found that their outward perception mattered more to me than any internal sense of self. I rarely felt anything but fear and an ever-pressing need to hide, to be safe. It was only after my autism diagnosis created a subsequent vacuum of social isolation and unemployment that the need to mask greatly diminished. I found I was far more concerned with 'myself' than I was with other people as I became beholden to none, and judged only by my own painfully constructed sense of self-hatred and self-loathing. Emotions I'd denied myself for a quarter of a century would surface, and empathy with TV characters' experiences I'd shared in a dissonant haze overwhelmed me constantly. When I realized I was non-binary, perhaps even trans, the image of a woman or the scenes of a girl living her life as a teen overwhelmed me with feelings of envy, even jealousy at times. Thinking back over those decades of passing as a neurotypical cisgender man, tightly constrained in expression and behaviour, I find a comfort in how numb I was back then. With an audience of one, I find myself far more judged than I ever was when I was passing to avoid judgement of peers, family or those around me socially. I am bordering on becoming bulimic, hate my physical form, and feel so deeply alone and lonely having lived someone else's life to survive. The painful cost of surviving over living is only now coming to dawn on me, no matter how necessary and important it was. Worse still, the act of passing grows harder each day, with each act of masking or scripting a hurtful betrayal of who I've become.

To be clear, I do not think an autistic non-binary person can be safe without passing. I can sadly never see a time that society will accommodate people like myself or welcome us. In many ways, this has only been validated and confirmed since my diagnosis, whether through personal experience or turning on the TV. Yet still I wonder who I could have been in another life, another time. Passing will hide you, it will keep you safe but it will never let you evolve your identity – that is the highest cost of spending a life on a stage. My journey continues down a path of the unknown, riddled with inaccuracies and fear that I will never find self-acceptance, never stop hating who I am or how hollow I feel. Tread lightly with those you counsel, support and aid, for they may be opening a Pandora's box of their own making and find themselves on this same path of confusion and pain that I now walk.

So little of the autistic non-binary experience is really known and I hope this small contribution helps to push the needle in the other direction. Given the impact and importance of the process of passing, its gendering within clinical circles and the use of passing as a scapegoat for the low levels of diagnosis of autism in women, it seemed a critical chapter to write. Please note 'we' are not 'one size fits all' and many things may be different from my experiences for the person you are working with.

Finally, it is important to remember that whether you are spending a week with this person or are going to be committing to years of support, you are but a chapter in their journey; but if you are a supporting influence, listen, and be realistic and open with them. The next chapter in their lives can be a more positive one, as more extensively discussed in Chapter 8. The world outside their door may be intolerable, and it may never be improved in their lifetime. What matters most to those that you work with is that you adopt their view of the world, whether in empathy or activism, and focus on what they need from you to improve their lives. It doesn't matter whether you feel validated, or they score you three points higher on their exit form. Unless you make a positive impact in their lives and give them somewhere 'safe' to be without judgement, rules or boundaries, how can you help them grow? I hope this chapter has given you some insight. You have a lot of work ahead of you. I encourage you to read, listen, open social media and see what actual transgender and non-binary autistic people are saying. I wish you well on your journey to help others and thank you for taking the time to read part of mine.

References

Kožnjak, B. (2015) 'Who let the demon out? Laplace and Boscovich on determinism.' *Studies in History and Philosophy of Science*, Part A, 51, 42–52.

Seth, A., 2017. *Your brain hallucinates your conscious reality.* [online] Youtube.com. Available at: <https://www.youtube.com/watch?v=lyu7v7nWzfo> [Accessed 18 March 2021].

Valentine, V. (2016) *Non-binary people's experiences in the UK.* [online] Scottish Trans Equality Network. Available at www.scottishtrans.org/wp-content/uploads/2016/11/Non-binary-report.pdf [accessed 13 March 2021].

Chapter 11

Doing Gender on My Own Terms

MY LIFE AS AN AUTISTIC TRANSGENDER WOMAN

Olivia Pountney

Introduction

In this chapter, I speak about my experiences as an autistic transgender woman, being transgender, the transitioning process and what support could have been beneficial during childhood, adolescence and into young adulthood. I use my anecdotes as a reference point for education for teachers, academics, health professionals, parents and fellow autistic trans people, specifically from a trans-feminine perspective. I hope that by doing this, I can help you understand a little more about what other autistic transgender women may be going through. I start by giving an overview of my experiences in my childhood and teenage years and how I presented very differently from what may be expected from a transgender child/adolescent. Then I talk about my experiences transitioning as a young adult, dealing with the barriers and forms of prejudice, particularly when it comes to how autism and neurodivergence are viewed, that could have prevented me from being able to transition. I also speak about my current perceptions on gender and how I see myself at this moment in time. Finally, I conclude with some advice about what would have been helpful to me, hoping to give you some tools to help other autistic transgender women to explore their own gender identity.

Experiences of childhood and adolescence

My earliest memory of experiencing gender dysphoria can be traced back to my pre-school days of being four years old. I remember being told by a teacher that the only correct way for a boy to use the bathroom was standing up and for a girl to be sitting down. This was the first time in my life that I remember feeling othered and ashamed for not conforming to how a typical boy should behave and act, but at that age I did not have the awareness or the acquired language to be able to tell myself who I truly was and nor would I gain this for some time. I regularly looked at myself in the mirror, not feeling complete or whole, as if something was wrong but without knowing what. I recall being perceived as a very difficult child at the age of four. I had outbursts and meltdowns that were usually triggered by things like difficulties with sensory aversion. As a result, I often ended up restrained by more than one person. I was very sensitive to the tone of other people's voices, perhaps more than my family and peers realized.

At eight years old, I was the complete contradiction of the stereotypical narrative of a what a closeted transgender child would behave like, but I was also a contradiction in what a boy was supposed to be. I was not into wearing pink dresses and secretly putting on my mother's makeup. Instead, it was videogames (particularly the Sonic the Hedgehog games found on the Sega Mega Drive), dinosaurs, space and ancient Egypt that occupied my time. I was infamous for arriving way too early for lessons on Tutankhamun, where I quickly gained the reputation for being a teacher's pet. In hindsight, I did display quite a few characteristics that have been associated with autistic cisgender girls (which might link to some of what Chapter 7 discusses), but of course nobody saw me as that when I was a kid. I was quiet, I was obedient, I paid attention. Boys, according to society, are both accepted and expected to be loud, boisterous and assertive. I was not any of those things. I was unlike the other boys in how I behaved and acted and as a result I had no friends apart from a very small group who were all fellow outcasts.

Throughout my childhood, I was constantly in an education limbo as I was in and out of specialist and mainstream schools, with little explanation given to me as to why this was. As a result, I felt very much like an outcast, as if I did not belong in either environment, and friendships that were formed were difficult to maintain. Ironically, I was always told the importance of friendship by my teachers and family but was not given the space to work on those friendships because of these circumstances. At the age of ten, I found out that I was autistic by watching the film *Rain Man* with my parents, which in hindsight hindered my understanding of autism. It sent the message that doing things that were considered autistic was not right, and in turn I internalized that my very being was wrong.

High standards continued well into puberty, as I was held to a much higher standard when it came to expectations than my classmates were. This is largely because I was in the middle of two different education worlds. Mainstream schooling considers academic performance to be the greatest priority; and special school considers 'fitting in' to be the greatest priority. I was internalizing two different classroom messages and agendas and failing to live up to these great expectations, which led to a lack of self-worth and belonging with my school peers. As I approached adolescence, my appearance, my body language – even as far as how I spoke (down to every word) – came under intense scrutiny from the teachers' terrifying gaze, while I saw boys of my age 'get away with murder'. The 'boys will be boys' narrative that allows boys and men to get away with a lot of problematic behaviours and actions did not seem to apply to me, despite being perceived as a boy.

At this age, I was still very sensitive to my surroundings. I was being sensory avoidant and struggling with people's tones of voice, largely due to my autistic brain, and this seemed to be perceived as 'unmanly'. At one point, it left me with no friends at all, and I felt that the only people whom I could relate to were people older than I was. I was told by the people around me that I was very emotionally mature and intelligent for my age. Unfortunately, this led to a lot of complicated situations where I became 'too attached' to those people.

I remember shutting myself away from the rest of the world when I first discovered body hair as a sign of my testosterone-dominated body morphing into the abomination that is the teenage body. My first sexual encounter was being on the receiving end of sexual assault. I suffered in silence for a very long time with no support, and this is something I have only recently been open about, largely because of the stigma associated with it, as well as delayed processing because of trauma.

No one had explained until I was around 15 what autism actually was and, more importantly, what autism meant for me, until I was moved to another specialist school after mainstream had failed to provide the appropriate support. Knowing that I am autistic helped explain why I had difficulties with socializing and sensory processing in a way that I could understand. It took a long time to get those answers and if I had been told from a younger age and given the correct support and tools, I believe my childhood would have been less traumatic.

During my adolescence, I struggled to relate to the experiences of boys and men around me. For example, I did not understand why it was so important to lose your virginity at a young age or why anger was the only form of emotion that was acceptable to express. For a long time, I assumed this was because of my autism diagnosis and the common autistic cliché of lack of theory of mind (not being able to relate to others through empathy, discussed in Chapter 2), but during this time period, I found myself relating to the struggles and experiences of girls and women. The (unfortunately still widespread) misconception that autism is a condition that only affects boys or men actually contributed to my not coming out as a transgender woman in my teens. Even now, I cannot think of anything that I could have said at that age that would not have 'othered' me from everyone else and highlighted my differences in an uncomfortable way. For the first 20 years of my life, I had learned not only how to mask elements of my autistic identity, but also my gender and queer identity, which in itself comes with a load of emotional baggage and trauma. I was particularly cautious of my body language and tried to avoid using effeminate gestures and to look as if I was unaware of myself and my surroundings. I tried to emulate neurotypical masculine presentations so that I could keep myself safe from people who would not approve of other ways of being.

During this time, and before coming out, I used theatre and amateur dramatics as a refuge for my gender expression. Not only was I able to express gender through applying theatrical makeup and wearing clothing that didn't conform to my assigned gender at birth, but I was given room to express a pallet of emotions that society frowned on me for expressing. It is somewhat of a stereotype that many people in theatre are queer, which is something that I also found to be the case for the most part, but I did not personally realize for myself until later. Gender can be and is, to an extent, performative, and we are all performers on a much larger stage, whether we realize it or not (as discussed in Chapter 2). Theatre helped me understand the process of using gender norms and expectations to interact with others, and thus helped me to gain an understanding of my own gender identity. Another helpful factor in the process of discovering my gender identity was my best friend. We had known each other since we were 11 years old and we supported each other when going through very difficult periods in our lives. We met through a local support group for teens and adolescents who are autistic, and we have been close friends ever since. In addition, we had many similar and overlapping interests and we have a similar set of values. She is like a sister to me. I felt safe being able to express myself around her, telling her about the more feminine aspects of my personality.

We had in-depth chats with each other about our sexualities and gender identities, which later lead to us coming out to each other. She came out to me as asexual and I came out to her as a trans lesbian. I remember that when I first came out to her, she did not seem surprised. I think that she was expecting it, based on everything we had talked about and what she had observed since knowing me. She was the first person that I came out to and when I asked her to call me Olivia and to use she/her pronouns, it felt right. She also helped me navigate feminine fashion in ways that were constructive and insightful but not patronizing and did not perpetuate harmful stereotypes onto me. I would tell her what look or style I was trying to pull off and she would give helpful tips. During the time where I was homeless because of issues with my family coming to terms with me coming out as trans, she convinced her grandmother to take me in until I was able to find a flat of my own. She helped me in more ways than she thinks and if it weren't for her, I wouldn't be here to tell you my story.

Transitioning

It wasn't until I was 22, when I had found the right words and the right communities, that I was able to say that I was a woman on my own terms, and only by my own terms was I able to accept that. Others, including family members, did not and still do not to this day. As a direct result, I was homeless for the best part of four months, relying on the help of a close friend to survive (the same friend that I mentioned above).

While I am grateful for the support that she gave me at that time, I think it goes without saying that I should not have been made homeless in the first place. During this time, it became clear to me that my family and society as a whole were trying to punish me for being trans. My local council suggested that I was placed in a men's homeless shelter, despite the fact that I was obviously not a man, and grossly overlooking the well-documented fact that trans women face high levels of violence in such places. In addition to it being a far from ideal living situation, I found it a horrifying thought that I could have faced such high levels of violence against me. As I previously mentioned, I was lucky to have a support network, albeit a small one, that was willing to advocate that I needed a permanent place to live.

Even in more 'benign' everyday interactions and situations, I felt as if the world had reacted negatively because they couldn't put a label on me when I had already found one. Before I came out, people called me a 'girl' and after I came out, people called me a 'man'. I believe that this was done with the intent of trying to disenfranchize me.

I am not sure whether coming out as transgender felt empowering to me, since transgender women are among the most disenfranchized groups in society, but it certainly felt right. It felt right when being addressed as 'miss' or being referred to with she/her pronouns. It felt as if everything I had experienced growing up made sense, when I struggled for years to piece it all together. It was like opening a window for the first time in years.

At 23, I had to seek hormonal interventions because my dysphoria was so bad. I travelled across the country to the centre of London to attend one-to-one gender counselling sessions with a therapist as part of pre-agreed conditions set by my former consultant to access hormone replacement therapy (HRT). The therapist spent most of the sessions talking about her nephew who, in her own words, had 'severe Asperger syndrome', rather than talking about me. She would make comparisons about how my autism was not as apparent as his, which made me feel incredibly uncomfortable, as I did not understand what being autistic in an 'apparent' way or not had to do with the validity of my gender identity. I should not have to mask or under-exaggerate my autism in order to be taken seriously. I did, however, have what I would call a 'passing paradox', where I could pass as a neurotypical-presenting person because I had developed coping mechanisms to make me appear less stereotypically autistic so that I could access gender-affirming care.

Gender-affirming care for me was a lifeline to deal with gender dysphoria but using so many of my resources to 'pass' as a neuro-typical came at a huge emotional cost of, and I became prone to burnouts. I think it unlikely that I would have been able to get the gender-affirming care that I needed if I had not been able to pass, so I feel fortunate that I could, despite this emotional cost. (Passing and its implications are discussed in Chapter 10.) Autistic burnouts are very common among autistic people, especially in adults, but from what I've seen, this very rarely gets spoken about outside autistic spaces and communities. Burnouts are often caused by the need to mask in order to meet the expectations of neurotypical people, whether that is for loved ones, for family members, to hold down employment or to get access to resources that we need such as food, healthcare, hygiene, social, emotional and recreational pursuits. This is a really unfair expectation to thrust on autistic people, setting us up for failure because, eventually, we will be unable to mask because of burning out. I am sure that I am not the only one who has found themselves in this situation with gender identity clinics.

Towards the end of 2017, my specialist retired and closed his clinic, leaving me briefly in limbo between service providers until the start of 2018. Thankfully, my GP, who afterwards admitted to me that she knew nothing about trans healthcare, wrote a letter to another clinic asking that I should be seen in the New Year and the request was granted. Even though I had been on hormones for a long period of time, I still had to go through much of the invasive questioning and scrutinizing measures by the team there to make sure that I was 'trans enough' to transition, including being asked about my sexuality. I think being autistic played a big part in why this happened. It was unnecessary and, in my opinion, probably a huge waste of time and resources that could have gone towards other priorities.

My current sense of identity and planning for the future

After four years on hormone replacement therapy (taking oestrogen supplements to feminize my body and testosterone blockers to suppress testosterone), eight sessions of voice therapy, countless laser hair removal sessions, a new wardrobe, and a facial feminization surgery, you would think that I would have travelled straight across the gender binary, from one side to the other or to be MtF (male to female), but this was certainly not the case with me.

As I started to pass as female to a lot of people, I found myself more at peace with my body and my mind. I could see and relate to my younger self, as if I had gone through a 'female' puberty rather than a 'male' one. By having breasts, a softer face and voice, it was as if I was entering a different world through the same eyes as my pre-teen self. I did not and will not travel in a straight line, but in a multi-dimensional space that somewhat represents a sphere. After all, how can gender be a simple line of belonging to one or the other, with a barrier between the two opposing binaries? After everything that I have been through, that simply does not make sense to me.

What I have discovered about myself through the 'process' of transitioning, is that I want to reclaim the older parts of my life, before

I started transitioning. The darker times of my life, where I found myself using theatre to mask myself, are now calling back to me. There is something incredibly ironic about standing on a stage and having a sense of newfound confidence. It is as if for the first time, I am at the mercy of people who see ME – not the person I was before.

But then, what I really wish people would understand about me is that I cannot discard the person who transitioned. I felt as if I was expected to metaphorically kill the person I was before I was Olivia. And, certainly, throughout my transition I wanted to. Now, however, looking back, I realize that who I am now and who I was before are connected. Every day I am discovering more things about myself and every so often my perspectives on gender do change.

That is why I would now say that I am a non-binary, trans woman. I am non-binary in the way that I perceive my own gender experience and presentation as something much more complex than the 'standard' male-to-female narrative. I did not transition just so I could be shoved from one box into another. I transitioned so I could be at peace with myself and ease much of the trauma that comes from dysphoria. I should be able to wear more masculine and neutral clothing if I want to and not be perceived as breaking an unbreakable oath. I should also be able to act in an 'unfeminine' manner if I choose to or have hobbies and interests that do not collate with femininity. In that sense, I am a gender non-conformist, even though I still feel a strong connection to womanhood. I want to be read as a woman to the gaze of strangers, even if I do gender 'wrongly' or if I don't live up to the expectations of patriarchal, cissexist femininity by, for example, not wearing makeup or having perfect hair. Being a feminist myself, I can easily see how these tropes are incredibly harmful not just to trans and cis women, but to everyone, and no one should be forced into such roles against their will. Furthermore, I am autistic. I always have been and always will be! Transitioning will never erase that. Consequently, being autistic will affect my perception of my own gender and how I choose to express it.

This also means that I simply cannot erase my own past. Digging up a grave for 'insert deadname here' is something that I just cannot do. The past 20 years of my life have strongly influenced the way I have interacted with the world and the experiences I have within it, whether they be good or bad, euphoric or traumatic. For better or for worse, they have made me the person I am today. Many of the communities that I was a part of, from my theatre groups and Doctor Who fandom communities, to autistic and LGBTQIA spaces, have been a part of both my past and present life, and all of these interactions have had a big impact on how I see myself. I still enjoy many of the hobbies and interests that I've had from childhood, as well as the newer hobbies I have acquired over the years, and I should not be expected to drop them just to please gatekeepers in whatever form they may take. I should be able to speak about my past life and how I feel about it without it being used to invalidate my gender.

My plans and hopes for the not-too-distant future include undergoing bottom surgery (in other words, to have a vaginoplasty). I have a lot of anxieties of having to go through more gatekeeping measures and having to justify almost every aspect of myself in order to get this. Furthermore, even if I am approved to have this, there will be a long waiting time to receive it. I find the constant gatekeeping of every aspect of the trans experience very draining and exhausting. Even in a best-case scenario, the actual process of having a vaginoplasty does terrify me, although getting facial feminization surgery has helped me somewhat to prepare for it.

Support that would have been helpful growing up (and may be helpful for others)

Given how repressive legislation like Section 28 (the ban on teaching homosexuality by local authorities) was enforced up until 2003, I think it would have been very hard for people to help me growing up without compromising their jobs and careers. Without getting into a deep conversation about upholding unjust laws and how such legislation largely affected trans people and their communities in general, being able to express how I felt about my body at a young age without the fear of ostracization from my peers would most likely have been very helpful for me.

In addition to being able to speak about my dysphoria, I think that gender norms should not have been so rigid both in a school and a home-like environment. Exploration and breaking of gender norms should be encouraged and not treated as a taboo. Having access to positive messages through things like personal, social, health and economic education and relationships education, and ultimately a curriculum that is trans-inclusive, would have helped. This also needs to extend outside the classroom and to be applied to a healthy learning environment. Gender-neutral facilities and zero-tolerance bullying policies that are actually enforced would also make a huge difference.

Having professionals with helpful attitudes around me would also have been very beneficial growing up. As discussed in many other chapters in this book, autism is *not a male/boy condition*. Anyone can be autistic, including the trans woman writing this chapter. Autism is not by any means a death sentence and many of us can and do lead fulfilling lives, but that does not mean that support is not needed. As someone who has experienced both sides of this extreme, on the one hand getting enough support because I can mask or appear 'high-functioning' and on the other being held back in life because I cannot function enough for mainstream society, I cannot stress enough that the needs of people like myself are much more nuanced than being high-or low-functioning. Just because I can mask and pass as neurotypical one day, it does not mean that I am not disabled by the world around me. And likewise, just because I had a meltdown or I have had a bad day when I can barely speak, it does not mean that I should be treated as a lost cause.

I have very complicated feelings about being in between mainstream and specialist schools, and the experience has left me traumatized to this day. At best, I felt as if I didn't belong anywhere, and at worst I went through a lot of abuse and neglect from those who were meant to support me. I feel as if there needs to be a complete overhaul in how our schooling system treats and supports autistic and disabled people, though I am not sure what this should look like. To be brutally honest, I think that schools shouldn't exist, because they are such horrible places. They can, however, be much better places if the people working in them are meaningfully educated, not just on inclusive policies but also on the Equality Act of 2010, ableism and cis heteronormativity.

The same should apply to many other institutions that both trans and autistic people access at different points in their lifetime. Unfortunately, transphobia and ableism interact with each other in many ways. Gender clinics in particular need to understand this and stop holding us to neurotypical standards that are difficult, if not impossible, to reach in order to access services and interventions that can help deal with dysphoria.

Everyone in society, including our families, loved ones, friends and support networks, can also help. Learning new names and pronouns can certainly help, but we are still the same person that you have known. How we talk about ourselves may change and what we come to expect from other people may change, but things like personalities, likes and dislikes, hopes, dreams and aspirations do not change. So, please do not act as if we are strangers, and do not mourn for the past.

Conclusion

In this chapter I have outlined my experiences of being autistic and transgender in the hopes that it will be interesting and informative to autistic transgender and non-binary people, their loved ones and those who support them. I cannot, of course, speak on behalf of an entire community of people, each of whom have different intersectionalities and walks of life, nor would I want to. Although we have come to the end of my chapter, my own experiences will most likely change over the coming years as well. If anything, this is not the end of my chapter, but the beginning of a far greater story. I have no idea, of course, what the future will look like, but I hope to revisit my perspectives in the coming years. I think it is worth remembering that all autistic transgender people are in the same place as me in that sense; they only know what their experiences have been like so far, and their identities and perspectives, like everyone else's, might change over time. Supporting and understanding them should be an ongoing conversation done with respect and open-mindedness, and I hope that my chapter has contributed to further expanding your own understanding of trans autistic identities and experiences.

Chapter 12

The Experience of Gender Dysphoria from an Older Autistic Adult

IMPLICATIONS FOR PRACTICE

Wenn Lawson

Introduction

Throughout this book on autism and gender variance, autistic individuals and others have written from our experience, as well as from reviews of the literature. We know our stories are varied and different because the autism spectrum hosts a variety of autistic experience which is unique to each of us. Although this lack of homogeneity makes it difficult to draw out generalized patterns, it is evident that the underpinnings of autism are common to all autistic people (American Psychiatric Association, 2013). Having said this, how we present and experience being autistic changes over time. As we age, autistic children, teens and adults face different challenges to when we were younger (Geurts, Stek & Comijs, 2016; Happé & Charlton, 2012; Lawson, 2015). Although this chapter is one story, from one older autistic adult, it is important we consider this story, because it gives us clues to what others might experience.

Autism changes with time because it is a developmental disposition. The *Diagnostic and Statistical Manual of Mental Disorders (5th edition) (DSM-5)* (American Psychiatric Association, 2013) refers to restricted and repetitive interests and connections to social communication, which imply that the autistic brain functions best when monotropic, being a brain that is 'wired' to use single focus (Lawson, 2011; Murray, Lesser & Lawson, 2005). This way of focusing is different from the broader focus found in the allistic (or non-autistic) population. A monotropic disposition invites many areas of strength and passion but also leads to various uneven strengths and delays. For most of us, unless connected to our interests, this implies difficulties managing 'change', multi-tasking, and staying motivated when not interested. For many of us, it also means that we prefer sameness, structure and routine (American Psychiatric Association, 2013). Being single minded, literal, ritualistic, resistant to change and naturally poorly equipped in social situations outside our interests can cause us, as autistic individuals, to believe we are inadequate as human beings. This negatively impacts mental health and self-esteem (Wiley, Lawson & Bearden, 2015). Applying the above to the job of 'knowing self', whether hardwired or environmentally influenced, may take us longer.

In the allistic population, gender identity is partly explained as a social construct where society expects behaviour from individuals according to their assigned gender. However, research shows that gender is also biologically wired; most children 'know' if they are male or female and happily choose traditional 'boy toys' or 'girl toys' accordingly (Todd *et al.*, 2017).

In this chapter, I present my own experiences as an autistic adult who transitioned later in life, at the age of 62. I will discuss how a variety of aspects such as poor interoception, lack of autism awareness and acceptance, misdiagnoses and mental health issues, as well as professional reservations, contributed to my late realization of my gender identity. I will also be discussing a range of implications of that late transition both for myself and my family.

Life before my autism diagnosis and gender transition

Growing up as an autistic transgender person in the 1950s and 60s, I did not have access to many of the resources and family support many young autistic individuals often receive today (e.g. for the different ways they process information and for their differing learning styles we have technology, visuals, role play, music). Because I couldn't 'read' the hidden curriculum of social interaction, I filled the gaps in my understanding with comic books and science fiction. Identifying as an alien and a mutant gave me a fictional population to belong to. I also loved certain television shows like *Lassie* and would imagine myself as the boy with his dog. I even dressed in jeans and baseball boots, just like the boy in the TV show. This felt right for me at the time, and today I believe this was more than simply identifying with a hero. It was an attempt to locate my gender identity. As an autistic child (undiagnosed at the time), I was unclear about many things, including appropriate ways to communicate. I adopted an American accent and lived daily life as if I were that boy. However, even though as children we may be able to get away with living as mutants, in a world we create, as we become adults this is no longer tolerated by family or the society that we live in. So, as we age, things can dramatically change. Losing access to the way I identified (a mutant), due to it not being socially acceptable, pushed me into deep depression.

Eventually, as an older person who was housed in a female body, I believed I was a 'butch' lesbian because of my affections for the female sex. I think it was forming this identity that kept me bound to the 'wrong' (for me) gender for such a long time. I never felt right using the label 'lesbian', but it was all I connected to at the time. Losing all the other ways I identified, however, meant that my self-confidence fell through the holes in the fabric of my life and the demands of life outweighed my ability to cope. This may account for some of the reasons some research shows autistic adults fare poorly in the workforce and their sense of well-being is lower that of the general population (e.g. Geurts *et al.*, 2016). We can also see this happen for individuals whose gender identity is different from that they were assigned at birth. To date, there is little research on autism and gender identity to help us understand the interrelationship they share. However, as we listen to adults tell their stories, we may get an idea of the extent of that connection and some of the reasons behind it. We know statistics on gender dysphoria appear to be higher in the adult autistic population, or those adults with autistic characteristics, by at least 6–7 per cent (Heylens *et al.*, 2018) when compared to 1 per cent of the allistic population.

Autism, gender identity and bodily signals

Connecting with and understanding one's bodily signals is vital in the process of understanding gender identity. One of the reasons why it took me so long to understand my own gender identity was my poor interoception. Interoception, the eighth sense that lets us know when we are tired, hungry, thirsty, sexually aroused, hot, cold, anxious, in pain, and so on, is often naturally offline in autism, as discussed earlier in this book (Chapters 7 and 9). Without connection to this very important sense, gender identity may be less well established. As a younger person, I battled daily with many interoceptive connections, which led to boundaries of my bodily experiences, such as knowing where my body began and ended, being difficult to work out. To help me 'feel' a greater connection, I wore a sports cap, for example, so I knew where my head was and how much space there might be between my head and a doorway. If, via my interoceptive sense, I had been able to notice the feeling of me and had been able to judge distance, I would have seamlessly known how to clear the distance between open door space and my 'beingness' and would have walked through that space without worry.

Having good interoception is vital for self-regulation and self-awareness. Self-regulation is dependent on reading body emotions and understanding them. At that time, however, I was not picking up on those signals early enough to notice anxiety building up, or anger and frustration, so it felt as if they were suddenly there, and my overwhelming response was to explode or implode.

Because I was not connected to understanding what I felt or what I needed, I depended on others to know for me. Throughout childhood, I rarely noticed others and did whatever came to mind, often inappropriately. This got me into lots of trouble. In my early and middle adult years, I grew to become co-dependent with my partner (Lawson & Lawson, 2017). I could not decide what I needed to do, and had to check-in on many other decisions a lot of the time. It was as if I could not trust myself to get it right. Some of these things changed dramatically after I transitioned from female to male (Lawson & Lawson, 2017). I believe that it is possible that having testosterone (the right hormone for me) coursing through my body helped connect my senses. Maybe due to being more confident (because I was joined up), I attempted more things on my own, which led to needing to depend less on others. I know my interoceptive sense still needs working on, but being at home with who I am has given me a good start. It might be that because I was not in the right body for such a long time, I had dissociated from that body, which only increased my lack of interoception and increased my need for co-dependency. It is also possible that the co-dependent relationship(s) had delayed the connection to my own gender identity.

It is difficult to separate gender and autism in as much as they both dictate who I am. For me, being autistic (it is different for everyone) impacts on how I process information. For example, I am slow in working out the spoken words in a conversation, as well as the body language people utilize to add value to their conversations. Recognizing faces is difficult and I often look for an item of jewellery or a certain haircut to help me build familiarity. It takes time to respond to others, and it is almost impossible to process conversation in noisy environments. This all impacts on my social interactions with others. For example, it is uncomfortable when a friend wants me to go out to a bar with them if that venue is noisy, and I need to say it is too uncomfortable for me. I am fine in quieter venues, but this is not easy to explain. I think my slowness to connect is why it took so long to join the dots in recognizing my gender identity. I knew I felt much more masculine than feminine, in the traditional sense of the terms. But I didn't know my detachment and my refusal to acknowledge certain female aspects of me (e.g. breasts, menstruation and my rounded female form) were associated with the term gender dysphoria.

I have a number of sensory discomforts that may be perceived as negatively impacting on my ability to communicate. This links to my gender identity in particular, because some tactile experiences (certain clothing) can feel like sandpaper on my skin, and items (e.g. buttons, zips, fluffy balls) can capture and take over my attention, making it nearly impossible to attend to anything else. Consequently, I need to wear soft and simple cotton clothing (such as T-shirts and track pants), which can appear non-feminine, casual, unfashionable, and so on. Since I was diagnosed as autistic many years prior to understanding my gender identity, for a long time I thought that my sensory response to clothes was bound up with my autism. Since realizing I am transgender, however, I have wondered whether it was more because these clothes were more masculine, and I felt more at home with myself when dressed this way. It has taken such a long time to realize that, for me, it's both.

My autism means I need to process things one at a time. I also struggle with concepts associated with object/person/emotion permanence (e.g. knowing something, someone or some feeling can still exist even if it can't be seen). These can be definite barriers to owning and living in the gender that is right for me. Because things shift all the time, I am constantly unsure of what is stable and trustworthy. Having a positive self-image and acceptance requires the individual to know themselves and to know what they like and do not like, as well as understand why. I found it very difficult to separate 'self' from 'other' and the fluidity of 'the other' seemed to flow on as part of me. Then, if that person left, I would lose all sense of self again. In many ways, it was not until I recognized my gender dysphoria and chose to transition (by changing my name and using male hormones and sex-affirming surgery) that I knew I was actually stepping into the trueness that was me. I only knew I was home when I got here!

Another factor that played a part in experiences of gender and transitioning was the way I experience emotions. I experience emotions as a 'colour' state rather than a 'feeling' state (a type of synaesthesia). This can seem odd when communicating with others. My sense of self was like a rainbow of colour before, and after transitioning this became anchored and less unstable. This enabled my mind to comprehend things more clearly and my sense of autonomy was further established. Those brown and grey hues of anger and depression were exchanged for more of the green of integrity and the turquoise blue of safety. I am reluctant to speak of these things with 'professionals' because if they were judged in the light of what passes for 'normal', I fear being thought of as 'mental'.

Mental health misdiagnoses

From the age of 17 through to 42 I was in and out of mental health facilities, treated for a misdiagnosis of schizophrenia. I spent years being medicated with a variety of harmful medications. This was a very dark time and one I am not keen to remember. Being 'in the dark' for all those years is not an uncommon experience for older autistic people, let alone those who also live with gender dysphoria. So many of us have been misdiagnosed with various mental health issues, such as social phobia, schizophrenia, social anxiety, borderline personality disorder and others, it is no wonder that depression and suicidality are so high among our population.

Having professionals listen to me and really hear me has been the most valuable tool. Being believed and then allowed or given permission to move into my masculine self has released me from uncertainty. The biggest barriers in many ways were my difficulty to connect with what was happening to me and my confusion in how to join the dots and to communicate or interpret what they were saying. Having the psychiatrist and psychologist help me make sense of my life was very useful. It is not that my autism and gender dysphoria were exchanged (one knocked out the other) once I stepped fully into the gender appropriate for me, but that being in the right gender illuminated and cleared away some of the debris that not being understood had caused. Once I could separate what was what, I found it much easier to own my areas of difficulty, accept the support I needed, and move with confidence into my masculine identity. My autism has not disappeared, but it has taken more of a step backwards because I am not so disconnected.

It has been interesting to experience a growing confidence in ways I have not known before. For example, since finding my home in being male, I am less ambivalent over daily decisions. I believe this is because I am more 'joined up' and this is allowing me to know more of my own mind rather than being torn by the opinions of others.

I still have times of indecision, but this is usually due to being over-loaded by demand.

Family

When I asked my daughter to sit down (because I wanted to tell her my decision to transition from being female to male), she said, 'I know, you are going to have a sex change, aren't you?' I was very surprised, and I said to her, 'Why do you think of this and not that I have some terrible ailment?' She told me that they (my children) had always known this about me. This may be one reason my children (in their late thirties and forties) have adjusted so well. My daughter and I never did 'girly' things together, like go shopping or see a 'chick flick'. I was always the autistic 'tomboy' type, very supportive with their studies, sport activities or interior décor that was needed in our home. So, to them I am Mum, just a man mum!

For my partner (now my wife) who married a woman (however butch), the journey has been very difficult. For her, it is as if I died, and her grief was overwhelming. My wife, also autistic, had much abuse growing up. Her concept of masculinity and men was born from fear, disrespect and anger. As we travel through these hurts and injuries together, a new concept is being born. Our relationship is founded on personal autonomy and commitment to each other's best. To date, my transition has been instrumental in her healing and in her coming to know, understand and accept herself. This is not an easy process, and many relationships would not survive, as ours has.

In conclusion, being an older person who happens to be autistic and transgender has afforded me the years to develop greater under-standing, areas of wisdom, more experiences, and a greater level of learning than when I was a child, teenager or younger adult. There are things I would like not to have travelled through, relationships I wish were still intact, and some regrets about the many mistakes I have made in my discovery of who I am. Some will say, however, that it is in our making of mistakes that we do our best learning. I still would rather not have made those mistakes, but I take hope from my learning and the insight I have gained. Self-acceptance is a journey that puts us on the right road, but it is only the start to a lifetime of discovery. Without it, our journey cannot begin, let alone be completed.

References

American Psychiatric Association (2013) *Diagnostic and Statistical Manual of Mental Disorders* (5th ed.) Arlington, VA: American Psychiatric Publishing.

Geurts, H.M., Stek, M. & Comijs, H. (2016) 'Autism characteristics in older adults with depressive disorders.' *American Journal of Geriatric Psychiatry*, 24, 161–169.

Happé, F. & Charlton, R.A. (2012) 'Aging in autism spectrum disorders: A mini-review.' *Gerontology*, 58, 70–78.

Heylens, G., Aspeslagh, L., Dierickx, J., Baetens, K. *et al.* (2018) 'The co-occurrence of gender dysphoria and autism spectrum disorder in adults: An analysis of cross-sectional and clinical chart data.' *Journal of Autism Developmental Disorders*, 48(6), 2217–2223. doi:10.1007/s10803-018-3480-6.

Lawson, W. (2011) *The Passionate Mind*. London: Jessica Kingsley Publishers.

Lawson, W. (2015) *Older Adults and the Autism Spectrum: An Introduction and Guide*. London: Jessica Kingsley Publishers.

Lawson, W. & Lawson, B. (2017) *Transitioning Together. One Couple's Journey of Gender and Identity Discovery*. London: Jessica Kingsley Publishers.

Murray, D., Lesser, M. & Lawson, W. (2005) 'Attention, monotropism and the diagnostic criteria for autism.' *Autism*, 9(2), 139–156.

Todd, B.K., Fischer, R.A., Di Costa, S., Roestorf, A. *et al.* (2017) 'Sex differences in children's toy preferences: A systematic review, meta-regression, and meta-analysis.' *Wiley Online Library*. https://doi.org/10.1002/icd.2064.

Wiley, P., Lawson, W. & Bearden, L. (2015) *The Nine Degrees of Autism: A Developmental Model for the Alignment and Reconciliation of Hidden Neurological Conditions*. London: Routledge.

Contributors

Marianthi Kourti

Marianthi is an autistic non-binary academic and researcher. During their MEd and PhD studies at the University of Birmingham, they investigated the experiences of autistic adults and how they form a sense of gender identity. They published on this topic in *Autism in Adulthood* in 2018. They also were an organiser of the 2018 conference 'Intimate lives? Autism, gender sex/uality and identity' and co-organized a series of workshops on the topic for the Participatory Autism Research Collective (PARC) as a West Midlands convenor. They are passionate about meaningful autistic participation in all aspects of autism research, advocacy and practice. They have worked with autistic people in various positions, such as Special Education Teacher, support worker and, most extensively, Specialist Mentor for autistic university students. After the completion of their PhD, they hope to research the links between barriers in autistic employment, their effects on mental health, and how they can be addressed with and for participatory autism research at the University of Edinburgh.

Damian E.M. Milton

Damian works part-time for the Tizard Centre, University of Kent, as a lecturer in Intellectual and Developmental Disabilities. He also teaches on the MA Education (Autism) programme at London South Bank University and has been a consultant for the Transform Autism Education (TAE) project and a number of projects for the Autism Education Trust (AET). Damian's interest in autism began when his son was diagnosed in 2005 as autistic at the age of two. Damian was also diagnosed with Asperger's in 2009 at the age of 36. Damian's primary focus is on increasing the meaningful participation of autistic people and people with learning disabilities in the research process, and he chairs the Participatory Autism Research Collective (PARC).

Shain M. Neumeier

Shain M. Neumeier is an American autistic transgender non-binary lawyer, activist, and community organizer, as well as an out and proud member of the disabled, trans, queer and asexual communities. Their passion on the issue of ending abuse and neglect of youth with disabilities in schools and treatment facilities stems from their own experiences with involuntary medical treatment and bullying, and led them to go to law school. They have pursued their goal of using legal advocacy to address these problems ever since. Shain's work appears in *Autistic Activism and the Neurodiversity Movement: Stories from the Frontline, Resistance and Hope: Crip Wisdom for the People, Rewire News*, and *Loud Hands: Autistic People, Speaking*. Among other honours, they were named the Massachusetts Bar Association's 'Outstanding Young Lawyer' in 2018, the Self-Advocacy Association of New York State's 'Self-Advocate of the Year' in 2017, and the Association of University Centers on Disabilities' 'Leadership in Advocacy Awardee' in 2015. When not working, they're probably crafting, playing Dungeons & Dragons, listening to history podcasts, or watching Netflix with their partner and three feline roommates.

Reubs J Walsh

Reubs J Walsh is a PhD candidate in Clinical, Neuro- and Developmental Psychology at the Vrije Universiteit, Amsterdam. They are also a non-binary, autistic trans woman. Reubs' PhD examines the role of the social environment and social-cognitive development in mental health risk, mostly in a community sample of adolescents, but also in autistic and trans populations. By examining how personal and social identity interact with cognitions, behaviours and the social environment to determine mental health outcomes, she develops theoretical frameworks intended to integrate across bioreductionist, (computational) cognitive and social levels of analysis.

They also enjoy collaborative projects investigating such diverse topics as the neuropsychology of political conflict, adolescent neuroendocrinology in social cognition, transgender mental and physical health, and clinical best-practice. After her PhD, Reubs will move to Toronto University to investigate how biopsychosocial processes related to sex/gender and stress may contribute to gendered differences in cognitive ageing and dementia risk.

David Jackson-Perry

David Jackson-Perry is a doctoral candidate at Queen's University, Belfast, researching autistic experiences of intimacy, sexuality and sensoriality, and has published several articles and book chapters in these areas. Various frameworks including critical autism studies, symbolic interactionism, and queer theory inform his thinking, and a firm belief in consultative and participatory research guides his methods. David is also a specialist in sexual health, and in his day-job he is a project manager in the field of HIV at the University Hospital in Lausanne, Switzerland. His focus is on improving quality of life for people living with HIV and combatting HIV-related stigma.

Taylor René Kielsgard

Taylor René Kielsgard is an autistic advocate, non-binary femme, and disabled mom of disabled adults. They are particularly passionate about addressing gender disparities within the autistic community, promoting access to reproductive and sexual health care, and ending sexual and domestic violence. Taylor holds leadership roles with several autism and disability-related organizations, and advises numerous research studies and community-based programmes focused on autism, gender, sexuality and reproductive health. They have given presentations and presented on panels at multiple conferences and universities, and advised federal agencies on disability policy.

Lydia X.Z. Brown

Lydia X.Z. Brown is an advocate, educator, and attorney addressing state and interpersonal violence targeting disabled people living at the intersections of race, class, gender, sexuality, faith, language and nation. Lydia is Director of Policy, Advocacy and External Affairs at the Autistic Women and Nonbinary Network. They are the founding director of the Fund for Community Reparations for Autistic People of Color's Interdependence, Survival and Empowerment, and the co-editor of *All the Weight of Our Dreams: On Living Racialized Autism*. Lydia is Adjunct Lecturer and core faculty in Georgetown University's Disability Studies Program, and Adjunct Professorial Lecturer in the American University's Department of Critical Race, Gender and Culture Studies. They serve as a commissioner on the American Bar Association's Commission on Disability Rights, and are chairperson of the ABA Civil Rights & Social Justice Section's Disability Rights Committee, board member of the Disability Rights Bar Association and representative for the Disability Justice Committee to the National Lawyers Guild's National Executive Committee. They also advise the Nonbinary and Intersex Recognition Project and the Transgender Law Center's Disability Project.

Isabelle Hénault

Dr Isabelle Hénault, is Director of the Autism and Asperger's Clinic at Montréal. She is a sexologist and psychologist from the University of Québec at Montréal, Canada. Her practice and studies have focused on providing diagnosis, education and support to children, adolescents, adults and couples living with autism and Asperger syndrome. Isabelle has developed a relationship and sex education programme, and works with individuals and groups to increase their understanding of sexuality and conducts relationship counselling. *Asperger Syndrome and Sexuality* was her first publication (with Jessica Kingsley Publisher in 2005). She is presently collaborating on numerous international research initiatives involving socio-sexual education, interpersonal relationships and gender identity. Isabelle is the co-author of *The Autism Spectrum, Sexuality and the Law* (Attwood, Hénault & Dubin) published by Jessica Kingsley Publisher, London (2014). In 2020 she co-authored a book on the Female profile of Asperger syndrome (Hénault & Martin), Chenelière Education.

Wenn Lawson

Dr Wenn Lawson, (Phd), AFBPsS, MAPS, AASW, autistic lecturer, psychologist, researcher, advocate, writer and poet, has passionately shared professional and personal knowledge of autism over the past three decades. He has written/contributed to over 25 books and many papers. Wenn is Associate Researcher with Curtin University (WA), Macquarie University (NSW) and the University of Southern Queensland, Tutor Practitioner with the University of Birmingham's (UK) Masters Autism course, a member of the autism Co-operative Research Centre (ACRC), Co-Chair of the Autism Research Council, Australia, Ambassador for 'I CAN', Australia, and is on the editorial board of Autism in Adulthood. Wenn is also a member of The ND Co. Australia, and a family man with autistic offspring and grandchildren. In 2008, Wenn won 4th place as Victorian Australian of the Year, and in 2017 he presented to the United Nations on matters of autism and ageing.

Ella Griffin

Ella Rose Griffin is an autistic university student with a BA in illustration. They are currently on a MA course for illustration, planning to do a doctorate in the arts. This will hopefully lead to a teaching or academic research job. They hope to write academic papers on autism to increase the amount of study papers that are relevant and meaningful to autistic people. They enjoy writing fiction, art and studying disability-related subjects in their spare time. They hope one day to see a film, TV series or book about autism made for and by autistic people and to create one of those things themselves.

Alyssa Hillary-Zisk

Alyssa is an autistic doctoral candidate in Interdisciplinary Neuro-science at the University of Rhode Island, and also non-binary. They refuse to choose just one area to focus on, but the overlap of queer and autistic experience is one of the areas they're interested in.

Jo Minchin

Jo Minchin is an autistic person, an autism parent (some of her adult children are also autistic) and an autism professional working for the NHS in her local Clinical Commissioning Group, where she has a strategic commissioning role; she also works with a number of Local Authority Partnership Boards. Her work involves her bridging the gaps between adult health and social care in the UK, and highlighting good practice. Her national work includes being Vice Chair of the Advisory Group for the All-Party Parliamentary Group on Autism (APPGA) and working with the National Autistic Taskforce. She has worked on the BASW Homes not Hospitals steering group, sits on the Operational Delivery Group of the Oliver McGowan Mandatory Training trials in Learning Disabilities and Autism, and works with the European Council of Autistic People. She has recently completed a Masters on autistic adults at the University of Birmingham, and has an interest in taking her academic studies further. Her works include studying the use of the word 'autism-friendly' in practice and the particular issues faced by autistic people in the role of 'Expert by Experience', as well as presentations on interoception and alexithy-mia. Her mission statement is that the human spectrum is wide and diverse, and we all have a rightful and equal place on it.

Lexi Orchard

Lexi Orchard is a non-binary autistic expert, passing for nearly 30 years as a cisgender allistic male. They were diagnosed late in life to safeguard their liberty after decades of misdiagnosis and confusion by medical professionals. They are a science fiction novelist and writer in the nonfiction areas of therapy, mental health and architecture, in addition to the intersection of passing in gender, sexuality, and autism. They continue to explore new dimensions to the autistic and transgender experience outside of academic channels in seclusion, herding cats and chasing overdue deadlines. Lexi recently gave talks on passing : 'The Complexities of Passing in a Hyper-Sexualized World' at the 'Intimate Lives? Autism, Gender, Sex/uality and Identity' conference in 2018 and 'The Problematic Nature of Forming Connections Whilst Passing' at Autscape in 2019.

Olivia Pountney

Olivia is an autistic service user who identifies as queer. She has been involved in the autistic advocacy movement in which she holds the belief that autistic individuals should have a bigger voice in the discussions around autism and autistic people, in a field that is largely led by parents and professionals. In addition, she has served on the committee of many autistic user-led projects and organizations, including Autistic UK. Olivia speaks about her experiences and interactions with trans healthcare providers, and with society in general, from the perspective of a trans female and some of the complications that have arisen as a result of being autistic. She hopes that her anecdotes can be used to help provide understanding of some of the issues that autistic transgender people face, specifically regarding access to trans health.

Index

Adams, N. 58, 62, 64, 75, 127
alexithymia 144–9
Allard, A.M. 50, 90
Allen, J.D. 94
American Psychiatric Association
    11, 92, 114, 117, 144, 177, 178
Anasa, Y. 55
applied behaviour analysis (ABA) 35–7
Aquilla, P. 100
Ardizzi, M. 143
Ashkenazy, E. 75
Ashley, F. 50, 61
Austin, A. 63
authenticity and safety tensions 58–60
autism
    conceptualizations of 26
    definition of 10–11
    diagnostic assessment for 97–101
    different experiences of 11
    double empathy problem 27
    and gender 16–17
    and gender dysphoria 108–22
    and gender identities 16–17,
        25–6, 49–50
    and gender variance 42–4
    interest model of 27
    intersection with transpeople
        and BIPOC 78–9
    and non-binary people 17
    secondary effects of 50–3
    and societal expectations 25–6
    terminology for 11–12
    and transgender people 17, 74–6
'Autism and the ghost of gender'
    (Davidson and Tamas) 93

Autistic Women & Nonbinary
    Network (AWN) 76
Auyeung, B. 55

Baio, J. 16
Bakker, J. 111
Barbeau, E.B. 53
Bargiela, S. 16
Barnett, J.P. 52
Baron-Cohen, S. 16, 42, 53, 55, 111
Barrett, L.F. 142
Bascom, J. 37
BBC News 17
Bearden, L. 178
Behavior Rating Inventory of Executive
    Function (BRIEF) 97, 103
Berger, I. 55
Berthoz, S. 144
binaohan, b. 77
bio-reductive theories 53
Bird, G. 51, 142, 143, 144
black and Indigenous people
    of colour (BIPOC)
    decriminalizing existence of 83–4
    defence of 81
    employment support 82
    experiences of authors 72–4
    in gendered spaces 82
    humanize experiences 80–1
    inequality recognition 82–3
    intersection with transgender
        people 76–9
    non-gendered support groups for 81
    as partners and collaborators 83

black and Indigenous people of
colour (BIPOC) *cont.*
practice advice 79–84
presume competence 79–80
trauma recognition 84
Blažev, M. 128
Bogdashina,, O. 100, 101
Bothe, J. 36
Bradford, N.J. 61
Brewer, R. 144
Bronstein, S. 36
Brooks, J. 40
Broome, M.R. 55
Brown, L.X.Z. 12, 36, 73, 75
Brown-Lavoie, S.M. 63
Burr, D. 57
Butler, J. 25, 28, 30, 62

Cage, E. 65
camouflage *see* masking
Cassiday, K.L. 144
Catmur, C. 144
Charlton, R.A. 177
Chater, N. 57
'Circles' exercise 102
cisgenderism 55
Coleman-Smith, R.S. 54
Collins, S. 77
colonial perceptions of gender 65,
77–8
Comijs, H. 121, 177
compromises by trans/non-
binary people 60–2, 63–4
conceptualizations of autism 26
Connolly, M.D. 15
conversion therapy 35–7
Cook, R. 144
Cornell, A.S. 143
Côté, S. 100
Craig, A. 142
Critchley, H.D. 142

Dale, L.K. 75
Dattaro, L. 107
Davidson, J. 17, 91, 93
Davies, S. 113
de Vries, A.L.C. 42, 51, 109
Delphy, C. 12
Devita-Raeburn, E. 35, 37

Di Monaco, J. 65
diagnostic assessment for
autism 97–101
*Diagnostic and Statistical Manual
of Mental Disorders (DSM- 5)*
(American Psychiatric
Association) 11, 117, 144, 177–8
disability justice approach 37–9
Dombroscki, B. 117
double empathy problem 27
Dunn, B.D. 143
Dworzynski, K. 16

Edmonds, G. 101
Einstein, G. 57, 59
Ells, C. 61

Fausto-Sterling, A. 13–14
Feldman, J. 65
Fletcher-Watson, S. 51
Flexible and Focused (Najdowski) 103
Fox, F. 37
Frewen, P.A. 143
Frith, U. 144

Gale Encyclopaedia of Psychology 91
Galluci, G. 90
Gebauer, L. 58
gender
and autism 16–17
colonial perceptions of 65, 77–8
as performance 25–6
and sex 13–14
gender dysphoria
assessment for 112
connections to autism 108–9
and interoception 114–15
and male brain 111
and object permanence 115–18
and obsessions 118–19
and older autistic people
120–1, 177–85
professional fear of mistakes 113–14
and safe spaces 120
and social environments 119–20
statistics on 109–10
and younger autistic people 120–1
gender euphoria 61
gender expression 66–7

gender fluidity 91–2
gender identities
   and autism 16–17, 25–6, 49–50
   autistic perspectives on 91–7
   and denial 94–5
   and diagnostic assessment
      for autism 97–101
   different expressions of 15
   and gender fluidity 91–2
   and interoception 114–15
   performance of 28–9
   practice advice 95–7
   and puberty 99–100
   research on 90–1
   and sensory sensitivities 100–1
   and sexual attraction 93–4
   as social construct 93
   tools for support 101–4
Gender Identity Profile
   (Israel & Tarver) 92
gender modality 50
gender policing 29–30
gender variance
   and autism 42–4
   definition of 13
   and interoception 141–3
   and sensory sensitivities 141–9
George, R. 16, 51, 63, 65
Geschwind, D.H. 14
Geurts, H.M. 121, 177, 179
Gioia, G. 97, 103
Glidden, D. 51
Godwin, S. 35
Goffman, E. 25, 28, 29
Golan, O. 55
Goodall, E. 114, 115
Goodman, R. 63
Graigg, S.B. 143
Grandin, T. 100
Grant, J. 77
Gratton, F.V. 75, 127, 145
Grey, N. 144
Guay, F. 128
Guerra, M.P. 113

Hackerman, F. 90
Hallady, A.K. 14
Hammer, J. 16
Happé, F. 144, 177

Harrison-Quintana, J. 77
Heasman, B. 27
Hénault, I. 91, 92, 101
Heylens, G. 108, 180
Hill, E.L. 144
Hu, Y. 43
Hurley, H. 109

In the Autistic Brain (Grandin
   and Panek) 100
intelligibility 64–5
interoception
   and alexithymia 144–9
   and gender dysphoria 114–15
   and mental health issues 143
   and older autistic adults 180
   as sensory sensitivity 141–3
interest model of autism 27
Israel, G.E. 90, 92

Jackson, K. 77
Jackson-Perry, D. 54
Jacobs, L.A. 51
Jalaja, J. 111
James, S.E. 63
Jones, C. 119
Jones, R.M. 37
Jones, S. 42, 91
Joseph, J. 36

Katz, J.N. 54
Kelly, G.A. 32
Kenny, L. 12
Khalsa, S.S. 142
Kinnaird, E. 144
Klabunde, M. 143
Klinkenberg, N. 143
Kourti, M. 16, 74, 91
Kozlowski, A.M. 16
Kožnjak, B. 160
Kristensen, Z.E. 55
Krystal, H. 144

Lai, M.C. 111
Lapidus, R.C. 142
Lavinas Picq, M. 78
Law, T. 76
Lawson, B. 122, 180, 181

Lawson, W. 11, 27, 114, 117,
    122, 177, 178, 180, 181
Lazarov, A. 143
Leinung, M.C. 111
Lesser, M. 11, 27, 114, 117, 178
Lettman-Hicks, S. 77
Liang, B. 58, 62, 75, 127
Life Magazine 36
Lorde, A. 74
Lovaas, O.I. 36
Lovaas Centre 35
Low, B. 36

MacLeod, A. 16, 74, 91
male brain in autism 111
Mandy, W. 16, 61
Markram, H. 42
Markram, K. 42
Martinez, G. 76
masking
    description of 155
    cost of 162–3
    impact of 156–62
    as tool for passing 154
    for trans/non-binary people 61–2
Matson, J.L. 14, 16
McNally, R.J. 144
Mendrek, A. 53
mentality of professionals 127–9
Milton, D.E. 11, 26, 27, 28, 31, 51, 62, 66
Mingus, M. 71
monotropism 27
Mottron, L. 53, 56, 57
Murad, M.H. 58
Murphy, J. 111, 144
Murray, D. 11, 27, 114, 117, 178
Mussgay, L. 143

Najdowski, A.C. 103
National LGBT Bar Association 77
Neumeier, S.M. 73
Newell, V. 65
Nix, S. 128
non-binary people
    authenticity and safety
        tensions 58–60
    and autism 17
    bio-reductive theories for 53
    compromises taken 60–2, 63–4

definition of 15
and gender identities 15
and high co-occurrence
    with autism 53–8
and intelligibility 64–5
masking for 61–2, 154, 155, 156–63
practice advice 64–5
and professional working 125–38
research on 53–4
as secondary effect of autism 50–3
and self-insight 58
support for 66–7

Oakley, A. 13
Oaksford, M. 57
Oberman, L.M. 121
object permanence 115–18
obsessions 118–19
older autistic people 120–1, 177–85
Olson, K.R. 58
Onaiwu, M.G. 75
Organization for Autism Research 101

Panek, R. 100
Pascual-Leone, A. 121
passing
    cost of 162–3
    impact of 156–62
    terminology of 154–5
paternalism 34–7
Paulus, M.P. 143
Pellicano, E. 57
Perez-Felkner, L. 128
performance of gender identities
    facets of 28–9
    and gender policing 29–30
    practice implications 31–2
    subversive acts 30–1
personal construct theory (PCT) 32
Pollatos, O. 143
Powell, G. 58
precognition 154–5, 156–7, 158,
    159–60
professionals
    fear of mistakes 113–14
    mentality of 127–9
    pronoun usage 129–32
    relationships with clients 133–7
    strategy development 129–33

pronouns 129–32
puberty 99–100

Ramey, E.M. 101
Ramey, J.J. 101
Raphaelito, J. 78
Raymaker, D. 71
Reardon, S. 111
Rekers, G. 36
Rice, C.E. 16
Rider, G.N. 61
Rivet, T.T. 14
Rood, B.A. 63
Rowling, J.K. 41
Rubio, E. 103
Rudacille, D. 114
Rüddel, H. 143
Rumball, F. 144

Sabbag, S. 144
safe spaces 120
Saito, T. 52
Saleh, N. 107
Sanbonmatsu, K. 114
Schandry, R. 143
Schmidt, C.W. 90
scripting
    cost of 162–3
    description of 155
    impact of 156–62
    as tool for passing 154
Sears, L. 50, 90
self-insight 58
sensory sensitivities
    and alexithymia 144–9
    and gender identities 100–1
    and interoception 141–3
Seth, A. 154
sex and gender 13–14
sexual systems theory 103
Shanks, M. 77
Sheppard, E. 27
Simmons, W.K. 142
Sinclair, J. 12, 71
Singer, J. 11, 112
Skewes, J.C. 58
Slater, J. 119
social environments 119–20
social gaslighting 142–3

Sorbara, J.C. 40
Soulières, I. 56
Sparrow, M. 75
Spencer, K.G. 61
Stanford, A. 101
Stek, M. 121, 177
Steward, R. 16
Stewart, C. 143, 144
Stokes, M.A. 16, 51, 63, 65
Stonehouse, M. 91
Strang, J.F. 42, 75, 89, 96, 102
Strauss, M.S. 57
subversive acts 30–1
*Supporting Transgender Autistic Youth
    and Adults: A Guide for Professionals
    and Families* (Gratton) 145

Tamas, S. 17, 91, 93
Tarver, D.E. 90, 92
Tateno, M. 52
Tateno, Y. 52
Tchanturia, K. 144
Thomas, K. 128
Tikuna, J. 77
Todd, B.K. 178
transgender children
    allies of 44–7
    experiences of 166–70
    and transphobia 40–1
    and youth liberation 39–42
transgender people
    and alexithymia 145–9
    authenticity and safety
        tensions 58–60
    and autism 17, 74–6
    bio-reductive theories for 53
    compromises taken 60–2, 63–4
    definition of 14–15
    experiences of 165–76
    and high co-occurrence
        with autism 53–8
    and gender identities 15
    and intelligibility 64–5
    intersection with BIPOC 76–9
    masking for 61–2, 154, 155, 156–63
    practice advice 64–5
    and professional working 125–38
    research on 53–4
    as secondary effect of autism 50–3

transgender people *cont.*
  and self-insight 58
  support for 66–7
  and youth liberation 39–42
transphobia 18–19, 40–1
Transitioning Together (Lawson
    & Lawson) 121–2
Trevor Project 36, 37

Valentine, V. 158
van der Meisen, A.I.R. 50, 109
Vermeulen, P. 143
Viecili, M.A. 63

Walsh, R. 53, 57, 58, 59
Warrier, V. 42
Wawrzyniak, A.J. 144
Weiss, J.A. 63
Werling, D.M. 14
Wiepjes, C.M. 113

Wiley, P. 178
Wilkinson, L.A. 16
Williams, A. 110
Williams, P.G. 50, 90
Winter, S. 52, 111
World Professional Association for
    Transgender Health 40, 41
Worton, D. 101

Yergeau, M. 28, 31, 75
youth liberation
  allies of 44–7
  and disability justice approach 37–9
  and paternalism 34–7
  responses to 33–4
  and transgender children 39–42
Yurcaba, J. 76

Zeitlin, S.B. 144